# Columbia

## Gem of the South

*Produced in cooperation with the*
*Greater Columbia Chamber of Commerce.*

～ *Photo by Suzanne McGrane*

# Columbia
## Gem of the South

*Editorial and Corporate Profiles by Chernoff/Silver & Associates*
*Featuring the Photography of Suzanne McGrane*

# Columbia

## Gem of the South

Produced in partnership with the Greater Columbia Chamber of Commerce
Donald McLeese, President
903 Richland Street
Columbia, S.C. 29201-2329

*Editorial and Corporate Profiles by Chernoff/Silver & Associates*
*Featuring the Photography of Suzanne McGrane*

Staff for *Columbia: Gem of the South*
*Acquisitions:* Henry Beers
*Publisher's Sales Associates:* John Tew, Robbie Wills, and Elizabeth Kibodeaux
*Executive Editor:* Ronald P. Beers
*Senior Editor:* Wendi Lewis
*Managing Editor:* Amy Newell
*Profile Editor:* Mandy Burbank
*Design Director:* Scott Phillips
*Designer:* Ramona Davis
*Photo Editors:* Ramona Davis and Amy Newell
*Proofreader and Editorial Assistant:* Heather Ann Edwards
*Contract Manager:* Christi Stevens
*Sales Coordinators:* Annette Lozier and Sandra Akers
*Accounting Services:* Sara Ann Turner
*Print Production Manager:* Jarrod Stiff
*Pre-Press and Separations:* Artcraft Graphic Productions

CCI

Community Communications, Inc.
Montgomery, Alabama

David M. Williamson, Chief Executive Officer
Ronald P. Beers, President
W. David Brown, Chief Operating Officer

© 2000 Community Communications, Inc.
All Rights Reserved
Published 2000
First Edition
Library of Congress Catalog Number: 00-022733
ISBN: 1-885352-77-8
**Printed in Canada**

∽ *Photo by Suzanne McGrane*

# Table of Contents

## Part One

## Part Two

*Photos by Suzanne McGrane*

# Foreword

Columbia is a Capital City. But more than that, we're a capital city — a great place to live and work.

From one of the top 10 zoos in the country to the oldest continually operating theater in America to hosting the U.S. Women's Olympic Marathon trials, there's always something to see and do in our city.

Columbia is home to a vibrant business community, and diversity is the key to our economy. The University of South Carolina, Benedict College, Columbia College, and other technical colleges are home to thousands of students, yet Columbia is not a college town. Fort Jackson is located in Columbia, yet Columbia is not a military town. Columbia has a sizable retirement community, yet Columbia is not a retirement city. Columbia's economy benefits from a varied commercial-industrial base.

Our thriving arts community, the beauty of nearby Lake Murray and the reawakening of our riverfront make today exciting and tomorrow promising in our town. In this book, you'll meet the institutions, the businesses and, most importantly, the people who make Columbia great. On behalf of the Greater Columbia Chamber of Commerce, I invite you to see all that our city has to offer and to see why we choose to call Columbia home.

*Jack Skolds*
Chairman
Greater Columbia Chamber of Commerce

*Photo by Suzanne McGrane*

# Preface

When I came to Columbia a little over 25 years ago, I discovered a city just discovering itself. As my adopted hometown begins the 21st century, I'm proud to say I live in ... a city just discovering itself.

Someone smarter than me once said the unexamined life is not worth living. Well, I believe the unexamined city is not worth living in, and by that measure, Columbia is the greatest city I've ever been in. From its founding as a central location for the state capital to, well, yesterday, Columbia has continually sought to invent, then reinvent, itself.

We stand, literally and figuratively, between two other wonderful South Carolina cities. One so reveres its past that it has turned history into a sort of civil religion. The other is equally obsessed with creating the future. We don't ignore either of those things in Columbia. But Columbians are very much concerned with today.

We're a city that is constantly trying to be better today—which is, after all, where we all really live. That's the essence of our efforts to create better schools, build stronger neighborhoods, support the Gamecocks and the Bombers, make art, see theater. Columbians aren't so concerned with creating a great city as we are with creating a great place to live.

Through these pages—or better yet, a visit—I think you'll agree that Columbia is a city well worth living in.

*Marvin Chernoff*
Chernoff/Silver & Associates

*Part One*

〜 *Photo by Suzanne McGrane*

# Chapter 1

# *Taking Care of Business*

The Columbia area has fostered a favorable climate
for business, with incentives that are attracting both national
and international companies. Columbia is on an economic
fast track—thanks to its prime location, business-friendly
government, educated workforce, and excellent
transportation system.

⌒⌒ The Columbia area has emerged as a premier marketplace for all kinds
of businesses. *Photo by Suzanne McGrane*

*Twenty-five years ago, business in South Carolina was rooted in four very traditional industries—textiles, tourism, the military, and government. In the state's largest northern cities, textiles were king; to the south and in Charleston, tourism and the Navy employed the majority of people. Columbia, the capital city, was primarily known for its military workers at Fort Jackson and as the largest employer of state government employees.*

What a difference a quarter of a century makes! In a matter of years, national and international industries started to take notice of something more than South Carolina's warm, inviting atmosphere. They recognized a stable, pro-business climate—one that included low property and corporate taxes, low utility rates, strong education systems, and a solid work ethic among the state's people. Enhanced by these economic attributes and led by a state government willing to work together with business, the Columbia area is now a premier marketplace for all kinds of businesses.

Greater Columbia emerged from this "Southern growth spirit" as a leader in business and industry. The reasons for Columbia's great business success can be attributed to a number of factors, one of which is geography. Conveniently located in the middle of the state, Columbia is now a center for manufacturing, trade, banking, insurance, and education, and it remains the top military and government employer in the state.

Columbia is also located about halfway between New York and Miami—a strategic position in the geographic center of the rapidly growing Southeastern market. The city takes advantage of this location through its highly accessible infrastructure. Columbia is one of just 11 cities in the nation with three major interstates. These vital roadways travel north to south, east to west, and northwest to southeast, with a major beltway connecting all three.

In 1997, the Columbia Metropolitan Airport, located six miles west of Columbia's central business district, completed a $50-million renovation, making it one of the most user-friendly airports in the Southeast. Passenger service is provided by seven airlines, with commercial cargo service handled by four airlines and a number of air freight operators. Columbia Metropolitan has more than 50 flights a day, and major destinations include New York, Houston, Cincinnati, Atlanta, and Washington, D.C. Two fixed-base operators also serve the Metro facility with various charter flights.

〜 (Right) The Sylvan Bros. clock, at the corner of Main and Hampton streets, has been a Columbia landmark for decades. *Photo by Suzanne McGrane*

〜 The Richland County Public Library has won praise for its unique architecture and light-filled interior. The facility's 20,000-square-foot children's area is one of the largest in the country. *Photo by Suzanne McGrane*

A full-service facility, the airport maintains a newly dedicated air cargo terminal, the Columbia Airport Enterprise Park (CAE Park), and Foreign Trade Zone #127.

United Parcel Service also selected Columbia as the site for its Southeastern Regional Air Cargo Hub. This translates to lower shipping costs, timely deliveries, and later pickups for businesses in the Columbia area.

New businesses and industry, expansion of existing businesses, and the presence of state government all contribute to the city's financial well-being. By 1998, the labor force had grown to 279,250, up from 253,090 in 1994. During the past decade, Columbia's unemployment averaged less than five percent, compared to six percent for the state of South Carolina and slightly more than five percent nationally.

Today, the region's biggest economic players are government, services, trade, and manufacturing. With an estimated economic impact of more than $100 million each year, the U.S. Army training base at Fort Jackson is a stabilizing factor, leading to high numbers of visitors and contributing to a strong retail economy. Education, too, plays an important role. Nearly

37,000 students attend the University of South Carolina, and a number of other colleges and universities in the city contribute to a thriving retail and service industry. Those colleges and universities, along with a strong technical education system, provide a growing labor market for employers as well.

A big advantage to area employers is the University of South Carolina's highly ranked Master's in International Business Studies (MIBS) program, which educates some of the country's top business students. As the first interdisciplinary, international business program of its kind, the MIBS program leads the way with a global approach to training business managers. It offers a core international business curriculum that greatly expands the focus of the typical MBA. Started in 1974, MIBS was developed in direct response to the demands of business leaders for managers who can live and work in the emerging global environment, who can speak at least one foreign language fluently, and who understand the nuances of culture in a particular country or region.

Today, the MIBS program has become a model, and it enjoys a growing reputation for excellence. The University of South Carolina has been ranked in the Top 10 in international business education for 10 consecutive years by *U.S. News & World Report* in its surveys of "America's Best Graduate Schools." As the program's reputation grows, so does the number of multinational companies seeking to recruit MIBS graduates. As an added benefit, the presence of these bright students who are knowledgeable and experienced in international business helps the Columbia area draw a wide variety of companies to the Midlands.

The Special Schools program at Midlands Technical College provides another beneficial service to the business community. Through this program, potential employees receive free training for specific jobs with new or expanding firms. Companies then can select new hires from this pool of trainees, which benefits employers and workers alike.

As Columbia enters the 21st century, the service sector is likely to lead employment growth among virtually all nonfarm wage and salary jobs. And in all areas, the employment rate in the Columbia Metropolitan Service Area (MSA) is expected to exceed that of the past decade. Currently, when secondary and part-time jobs are included, the Columbia MSA employs approximately one-fourth of all employable residents in the state. According to Bureau of Labor statistics, the number of jobs in the state of South Carolina will grow to more than 2 million by the year 2005, which in turn also will statistically increase the number of employees in the Columbia area.

Greater Columbia has a number of factors that make working and living in the region desirable. According to the *Wall Street Journal* in 1997, Columbia's cost of living was the lowest in the Southeast and the sixth-lowest in the nation.

Businesses are attracted by Columbia's low manufacturing wages, pro-business tax incentives, low workers' compensation rates, and low unemployment insurance costs. Columbia's numerous educational and

**⌒ The Confederate Soldier Monument is one of several monuments on the grounds of the Capitol Complex.** *Photo by Suzanne McGrane*

professional development programs strongly support employment training for jobs at all levels.

With so many advantages, it's no wonder Columbia has attracted so many international businesses in recent years. The city's strong selling points include not only an excellent business climate, but also a skilled workforce to employ. From larger companies such as Pirelli Cables and Systems L.L.C. and Bose Corporation to midsize companies such as Hueck Foils, Holopack International, and Lang Mekra, foreign investment in Columbia keeps growing. In 1999 alone, 13 foreign companies either expanded operations or opened new facilities in the area.

According to a senior executive at Bose, the company selected Columbia because it offers so much. The city's strategic location combined with a very desirable quality of life, as well as its superior labor pool, stable economy, and government were all factors in Bose's decision.

However, international businesses are only the tip of the iceberg in Columbia. Recognized by the *Wall Street Journal* as one of the best business climates on the map, this area is home to numerous U.S. Fortune 500 companies. Blue Cross and Blue Shield of South Carolina, Colonial Life & Accident Insurance Company, and MYND all have their headquarters in Columbia. In addition to business and industry, Columbia area hospitals employ more than 8,000 people, and the University of South Carolina and other

(Above) Columbia Metropolitan Airport enjoys a reputation as one of the most user-friendly airports in the Southeast. *Photo by Suzanne McGrane*

(Below) Golfers will find scenic fairways at area courses. *Photo by Suzanne McGrane*

Columbia's economic prosperity in recent years has created thousands of new jobs. *Photo by Suzanne McGrane*

area colleges collectively employ more than 7,000.

All this economic success can be attributed to something more than just a favorable business atmosphere and terrific weather. A commitment to business—demonstrated by economic programs initiated on city, county, and state government levels—brings significant benefits to the Columbia area. In addition, area development groups such as the Greater Columbia Chamber of Commerce and other area chambers of commerce, the Central Carolina Economic Development Alliance, and the state's Department of Commerce work in partnership with area governments in a collective effort to ensure Columbia's growth and prosperity.

Numerous representatives from this area have traveled throughout the United States and Europe to spread word of Columbia's economic opportunities. The results have been well worth the effort, with thousands of new jobs and capital investments topping $1 billion annually in recent years.

According to Robert V. Royall Jr., former secretary of commerce for South Carolina, an economic development plan must be a cooperative effort between the community, its businesses, regional development groups, and the government. The fact that so many companies have chosen to locate in the Columbia area proves the plan is working. ◘

**Columbia's leaders realize a strong educational system creates a better future for youngsters and the entire community.** *Photo by Suzanne McGrane*

**(Right) The largest plant and produce market in the Southeast can be found at the State Farmers Market on Bluff Road.** *Photo by Suzanne McGrane*

# Galeana Chrysler-Plymouth-Jeep-Kia

The Galeana Automotive Group, 30 years ago no more than Frank Galeana's ambitious dream, is now one of the largest dealership chains in the country. Its Columbia location is one of Chrysler's brightest stars, literally, as the only dealership in the Midlands to achieve the coveted "Five Star" certification.

This certification, earned in 1998, signifies leadership in sales, customer satisfaction, repair quality, and ongoing process improvement. These characteristics have long been recognized by Galeana's customers in Columbia, who have seen firsthand the dedication of Galeana's staff to service and consistency.

Galeana's enthusiasm for serving the people of Columbia extends beyond the showroom and body shop. It supports many local charities, including the United Way, the Boy Scouts, and Palmetto Place, a shelter for abused children. Galeana is a strong leader in the Columbia community and looks forward to a bright future both for our business and for the community.

# Benedict College

Benedict College has attracted many successes that speak to its spirit and quality. The average SAT scores, Honors College enrollee rate, capital giving dollars, and the number of research grants awarded to Benedict College have all increased. Also growing are the numbers of valedictorians and high achievers making the school their first choice for higher education.

"Benedict College has proven, over the years, its ability to be a leader and to create leaders. Right now Benedict is on the threshold of a new and exciting era in its existence. Academically, we are positioning this college to be the best in its class nationally. We are also positioning this college to provide real solutions to societal problems. And we are positioning this college to be a source of visionary leaders for our state and our nation."

—*Dr. David H. Swinton*
President of Benedict College

# *Colonial Life & Accident Insurance Company*

While Colonial Life & Accident Insurance is one of the premier providers of employer-sponsored, voluntary employee insurance products in the nation, it is also committed to its employees and to community service. And this commitment trickles down from the top. The leadership of Colonial is just as committed to putting people first—employees and those in the community—as are all of Colonial's employees.

Bob Staton sets a great example through his personal involvement in the community. He leads community-based education reform initiatives built on partnerships between leaders in education, business, and the public sector through his involvement with the Education Oversight Committee, the Alliance for Excellence in Education, and the PASS (Performance and Accountability Standards for Schools) Commission.

"We support the community by trying to make it better in terms of education, family issues, the arts, public health, and economic development," Staton says.

## *Columbia Metropolitan Airport*

Whether taking off or touching down, travelers will find a wonderful atmosphere at Columbia Metropolitan Airport. The airport staff takes great pride in the recently remodeled facility, and employees strive to make every visitor's journey a pleasure. New architectural features include blue tinted glass and domed skylights, giving the airport a perfect look for the 21st century. The renovation has brought many "user-friendly" amenities such as a new food court, moving sidewalks that lead to the two-level concourse, and a completely refurbished terminal. United Parcel Service has selected the airport as home for its Southeastern freight hub, and several major air carriers provide a variety of destinations for the traveling public. Today, the airport serves more than one million passengers a year. To accommodate this growing client base, Columbia Metropolitan will continue its mission—to provide service that's "above and beyond."

# USC College of Engineering & Information Technology

Creative visions are taking shape at USC's College of Engineering & Information Technology—visions that will bring a brighter future to South Carolina. Today, economic progress is directly tied to high-tech advances, and the College of Engineering & Information Technology is expanding students' technological horizons. The college offers programs in chemical engineering, civil and environmental engineering, electrical engineering, computer science and engineering, and mechanical engineering. Business, industry, and government all benefit when these highly skilled graduates enter the workforce. In addition, the College has launched a High Technology Incubator, which offers support to new, high-tech small businesses. Emerging companies are nurtured through their vulnerable start-up phase, and the program supplies business owners with the tools they need to succeed. It's one more way that the College of Engineering & Information Technology is building a better tomorrow.

# Chapter 2

# A Capital City From The Start

The city of Columbia was established in 1786 for a single purpose—to serve as the new capital of South Carolina. Residents carefully planned their community and established a tradition of civic pride that continues to this day.

↜ **Columbia's Capitol building has undergone a multimillion-dollar renovation, including restoration of the copper dome.** *Photo by Suzanne McGrane*

*In 1791, a visitor remarked that although Columbia was "laid out on a very large scale," it was "now an uncleared wood with very few houses in it." This visitor was President George Washington, and he was right—both about the city's ambitious size and about its frontier-town appearance. But after all, at the time of Washington's visit, South Carolina's capital city was a mere four years old.*

While both the upstate and the low country of South Carolina already had become heavily populated by 18th-century standards, the Midlands remained largely unsettled until the town of Columbia was established in 1786 by an act of the state's General Assembly.

Columbia was founded for the express purpose of serving as the state's capital. Charleston, South Carolina's oldest and then-largest city, had been the capital under British rule, but upstate residents were not happy about being so far removed from the seat of political power. Discussion about moving the capital began almost as soon as the colony won its independence, and various sites were proposed. Many Charleston legislators opposed the idea of a move altogether, but in March of 1786, Sen. John Lewis Gervais introduced "A bill for removing the seat of government from Charleston." It was proposed that the new capital be located on the banks of the Congaree River, just down from where that river was formed by the merging of the Broad and Saluda rivers. This site was deemed appropriate primarily because of its location in almost the exact geographic center of the state. After much discussion, the bill was passed, and by a close vote, Columbia was chosen over Washington as the town's name.

Some of the legislators expressed doubts that Columbia, situated in the backwater between the two most populous regions of the state, would ever attract a large number of residents. Nevertheless, it was decided the town should be designed with care. Consequently, Columbia has the distinction of being one of the nation's first planned communities. The legislature recognized that the establishment of a new community from the ground up afforded them a rare opportunity to make careful decisions about such matters as the layout of streets and the development of neighborhoods. They decided the town's streets should be wide and straight and that lots, both residential and commercial, should be spacious. Pierre L'Enfant, who designed the layout of Washington, D.C., was selected to oversee the project. A square parcel of land, two miles on each side, was surveyed and laid out accordingly. Lots were offered for sale by September of 1786, but the town's roads were not actually constructed until 1787. By 1788 almost 50 houses were under construction.

As George Washington observed, Columbia did not become a bustling city overnight, but the foresight of the city's planners would serve it well over the years. Its wide streets and square layout, adopted as a means of providing relief from the area's hot climate, have made Columbia that rarity among modern metropolises: a city whose downtown is truly easy to negotiate by car. These features also give modern Columbia a feeling of spaciousness that is unusual today in urban communities.

In 1789, construction began on Columbia's first State House, and the General Assembly met there for the first time in 1791. The original wooden structure was located on the grounds of today's State House.

The town had its first newspaper, the *Columbia Gazette*, by 1791, its first church by 1794, and its first school by 1795. By 1797, mail was carried between Columbia and Charleston twice a week when the Legislature was in session. And by 1801 the town had its first jail.

〜 **Trinity Episcopal Cathedral, located on Sumter Street, is a replica of York Minster Cathedral in England.** *Photo by Suzanne McGrane*

Columbia's population still was small, and it lacked many of the amenities of more established cities such as Charleston, but in 1791 more than 150 people attended a lavish dinner in President Washington's honor. And even if Washington thought Columbia looked a little rough around the edges, he still was impressed with many things. In fact, he was so impressed with the new State House that he suggested its young architect, South Carolina native James Hoban, should help design the new national Capitol building that was under construction at that time. As an added distinction, Hoban was ultimately selected as the architect for the White House.

By the turn of the century, Columbia only boasted about 200 houses and 10 retail stores. But the small community's location in the middle of the state once more proved to be a boon when, in 1801, the legislature decided to make Columbia the home of the new South Carolina College. Tensions between the upstate and the low country were still running high, so, upon proposing the college, Gov. John Drayton promised that "the friendships of young men would thus be promoted and strengthened throughout the State, and our political union much advanced thereby." The college's central location in Columbia made it possible for young men from different parts of the state to meet each other halfway. The General Assembly set aside $50,000 for the school, which admitted its first students in 1805.

Columbia was now both the political and intellectual center of South Carolina life, and it began to grow accordingly. New churches were founded every year—among those still in existence today are First Presbyterian (1795), First Baptist (1807), Trinity Episcopal (1812), St. Peter's Roman Catholic (1824), and Ebenezer Lutheran (1830). The second bookstore in the state opened in Columbia in 1816, which was also the year the town got its first fire department. In 1825, the Marquis de Lafayette made Columbia a stop on his famous tour of the United States; he visited for three days and was lavishly feted. When noted orator Daniel Webster visited Columbia in 1847, he was very impressed, remarking that "the situation

and the town are very beautiful" and that the college "is flourishing."
Another visitor described Columbia as "a vast village of old-time planters'
houses, with their heartsome shades, large verandas, wide halls, climbing
flowers, and vines, and with the live-oak to cool the streets and the ever-
blossoming magnolia to perfume the attribute," and concluded that it was
"the favored city of the South."

Every accolade gave Columbians good reason for civic pride, which they
possessed in abundance. Residents always were eager to show off their
community to visitors, and the town's early history is filled with records of
parades, balls, and dinners celebrating milestones in Columbia's history.

꡸ **Striking architecture is a hallmark of homes in Shandon's Wales
Garden area.** *Photo by Suzanne McGrane*

꡸ **(Left) The DeBruhl Marshall House on Laurel Street was built in
1820.** *Photo by Suzanne McGrane*

꡸ **(Next page) Construction on Columbia's State House began in
the 1850s, and the structure was not complete for more than 50 years.**
*Photo by Suzanne McGrane*

The arts began to thrive in Columbia in the first part of the 19th century, too, and the city witnessed its first opera in 1799 and had its own theater by 1826. In 1841, South Carolina College became the first college in the country to have a library that was housed in its own building. And, lest the students be distracted from their studies, the city government passed a law prohibiting the establishment of "bawdy and gaming houses" within a 10-mile radius of the college.

All of these developments made Columbia increasingly resemble a true city. And the town's cosmopolitan flavor got an added boost in 1856, when work was started on an impressive new State House. But Columbia's real growth spurt came about not as a result of its social or political climate, but for economic reasons. Much to the surprise of residents of other parts of the state, the little town founded to keep peace between the upstate and the low country became a giant in South Carolina's burgeoning cotton industry. By 1820, South Carolina was producing more cotton than any other state in the nation, and much of it passed through Columbia on its way to markets all over the world. As it grew into an important commercial center, Columbia gained new residents by leaps and bounds. In 1830 its population was 3,310. Within a decade, this number grew by almost 25 percent to 4,340. In 1850 more

෴ **Main Street was only a dirt road in Columbia's horse-and-buggy days.** *Courtesy of South Caroliniana Library, University of South Carolina, Columbia*

෴ **(Left) A statue on the State Capitol grounds honors Wade Hampton, South Carolina's governor from 1876 to 1879.** *Photo by Suzanne McGrane*

than 6,000 people called Columbia home and, on the eve of the Civil War, the city's population had reached 8,052.

As befitted the denizens of a capital city, Columbia residents evinced a spirited devotion to politics, both local and national, from the town's earliest days. The fervor with which Columbians followed national elections and celebrated victories of favored candidates suggested they were fiercely patriotic and loyal U.S. citizens. But in fact, as early as 1830, there was growing dissatisfaction about national economic policies among South Carolinians, and in September of that year, Columbia was the site of a states' rights meeting. By 1832 there was serious talk of leaving the Union, which culminated in a nullification convention. Most Columbians opposed nullification, and the matter eventually died down. But, Southerners' frustrations continued to grow, fueled by restrictive federal tariffs that hurt the region's agrarian economy.

By the late 1850s, tensions between Northern and Southern states were running high, and talk of secession once more dominated political discussions in South Carolina. This time, the majority of citizens were in favor of leaving the Union, and after Lincoln was elected president in 1860, a Secession Convention was held at Columbia's First Baptist Church. A local smallpox outbreak was the only thing that prevented Columbia from becoming the site where the resolution was announced that began the Civil War. When news of the outbreak reached the conventioneers, they hastily reconvened in Charleston, where, on December 20, 1860, they voted unanimously to withdraw from the Union. Because South Carolina was the first state to secede, Columbia was, however briefly, a national capital—the political center of a state that had just become a nation unto itself.

But other Southern states soon followed South Carolina's lead, and the first battle of the Civil War took place in April 1861 at Fort Sumter in Charleston. Columbia soon became the site of military training camps, a prisoner-of-war camp, a military supply depot, a military hospital, and numerous new manufacturing concerns that produced everything from gunpowder to socks and buttons for the Confederate Army. Columbia's importance to the Confederacy caused its population to swell from 8,000 to 25,000 in just four years. But despite all the new jobs created by the war, these years were hard for most Columbians. Much of the city's male

∽ **The Gervais Street Bridge spans the Congaree River and leads into the Vista, Columbia's revitalized warehouse district.** *Photo by Suzanne McGrane*

∽ **(Left) Eau Claire town hall, which houses the north region police substation, has been restored to its former glory.** *Photo by Suzanne McGrane*

population was in the Confederate Army, and casualties were high. Skyrocketing inflation and shortages of many food staples meant that few of those who remained at home were able to live comfortably.

But these hardships were just a taste of what was to come.

In February 1865, Gen. William Tecumseh Sherman and his troops marched north from Savannah and set up camp just west of Columbia on the banks of the Congaree. Almost immediately, they began to shell the city. Some of their shells struck the still-unfinished State House, and today these places are marked with bronze stars. In an attempt to keep the Union Army out of the city, the Confederates burned all the bridges into Columbia, but Union Army engineers built a pontoon bridge across the Congaree, and on the morning of February 17, Union troops swarmed over it. By nightfall, Columbia was in flames. When the fire was over, much of the city—especially

✍ **The downtown area is home to several bed-and-breakfast establishments.** *Photo by Suzanne McGrane*

Carolina College, newly renamed the University of South Carolina, resumed classes in 1866. In 1870 Benedict Institute and Allen University both opened their doors, offering educational opportunities to recently emancipated African Americans. Construction revitalized the city and included the erection of a new city hall in 1874. Some political tensions were inevitable in the postwar era, but Columbia's leadership sought to pursue a moderate course. By the mid-1870s, both the city and the state enjoyed stable government by popularly supported leaders.

In the 1880s, the city's economy once more began to look robust. Banking became a major enterprise, and several new textile mills were built in or near the city. Columbia got its first streetcars in 1882 and its first public school system in 1883. And the city's central location became an asset to its retail economy, as residents from all over the state traveled to Columbia to do their shopping.

Public schools and public transportation led to further population growth and residential development. Although they are now considered part of the city proper, neighborhoods such as Eau Claire, Wales Garden, and Shandon were all new suburbs in the late 19th and early 20th centuries. Young people from these neighborhoods would ride the streetcars into town for dates and dances. And by the early 1900s, Columbians could entertain themselves by watching the city's own professional baseball team or attending movies at one of three local theaters.

When war again loomed on the horizon in 1917, Columbia once more played an important part in the war effort. Camp Jackson, on the outskirts of town, was established just after the United States entered World War I, and in the next year, 70,000 soldiers were trained there. Columbians followed national and international politics with particular concern at this time because President Woodrow Wilson was something of a native son, having spent his teenage years in Columbia.

After the Treaty of Versailles ended the war in 1918, Camp Jackson was closed. Columbians became eager to put the memories of war behind them and embrace the spirit of the 20th century. Although few of the city's streets were paved, automobiles became all the rage. The city's utilities got a major boost when the South Carolina Electric and Gas Company built a dam across the Saluda River to harness hydroelectric energy. The Saluda Dam was completed in 1930 and was the largest earthen dam in the country at the time.

Columbia's first radio station, WBRW, began broadcasting in 1929,

the downtown commercial and residential districts—had been destroyed. Whether Columbia was burned on Sherman's orders or whether drunken soldiers started the blaze accidentally is unclear, but the fire remains one of the most momentous and haunting episodes in the city's history.

After the war, the rebuilding process was slow and difficult for Columbia. Reconstruction saddled the city with an $850,000 debt that took years to repay. But, today's State House building opened in 1865, and South

followed in 1930 by WNOK-TV, which still serves the area today as WLTX. Popular entertainers such as Will Rogers made appearances in the capital city throughout the 1920s. Owens Field, Columbia's first airport, opened in 1929, and construction began on the Township Auditorium, which is still in use. And the city's population continued to grow rapidly, almost doubling from 26,319 in 1910 to 50,581 in 1930.

Prohibition did little to dampen residents' spirits; most Columbians simply ignored the new law and purchased alcohol from bootleggers or manufactured it at home. But hard times loomed ahead for Columbia, just as they did for the rest of the nation. The Great Depression was presaged in South Carolina by falling cotton prices that plagued the state's farmers throughout the 1920s, resulting in many bank failures. When the Depression hit, Columbia fared better than many cities because it was home to a number of government agencies that provided jobs for many residents. Government construction projects also added to the city's

infrastructure—by the decade's end, the university had new dormitories, a new library, and a football stadium, and the city had a veterans hospital and a new farmers market.

A year after war broke out in Europe in 1939, Camp Jackson—renamed Fort Jackson—was reactivated, and thousands of soldiers were in training there. After the bombing of Pearl Harbor forced the United States into the war in 1941, Fort Jackson and other local military installations took on particular strategic importance. It was at the Columbia Army Air Base that Colonel Jimmy Doolittle prepared his men for the 1942 air raid on Tokyo that became a turning point in the war. And in June of 1942, British Prime Minister Winston Churchill visited Fort Jackson to see how the Americans were training their soldiers.

⌒ **Ornate architectural details adorn the SouthTrust Bank building, located downtown.** *Photo by Suzanne McGrane*

This time, Fort Jackson was not shut down after the war ended. It remains in operation today and is one of the largest army training facilities in the nation. Fort Jackson also brought yet more people to Columbia and was one reason why Columbia surpassed Charleston as South Carolina's largest city in 1950.

In the following decades, the Columbia area saw more growth. Many new businesses came to the region in the 1950s and 1960s, citing the location, inexpensive utilities, stable political climate, and healthy labor market as reasons for their choice. When a modern new jetport opened in the early 1960s, Columbia became even more attractive to business leaders.

In 1965, Columbia was—for the second time—named an "All American City." Its farsighted city planning, concern with historic preservation, and successful implementation of desegregation earned it national attention as a model representative of the New South. Another thing that certainly made Columbia a representative Southern city was its growth; like so many other cities in the region, it experienced a population explosion that started in the 1960s and shows no sign of abating to this day.

It was in the '60s that Columbia's population first exceeded 100,000. But unlike some neighboring cities, Columbia was, by and large, prepared for such growth. Urban planning was a priority for community leaders throughout the 1960s. Their awareness of the consequences of growth led to the development of an infrastructure—new roads, new schools, new subdivisions—that could accommodate the massive influx of new residents.

For much of Columbia's history, most of its residents were South Carolina natives. In recent decades that has changed. Today, people from all over the country—and from all over the world—call Columbia home. These new inhabitants add a cosmopolitan flavor to a city that always has been characterized by traditional Southern charm.

Modern Columbia truly does offer something for everyone. As a capital city that is home to a major research university, a large military base, a booming business sector, and a thriving arts community, Columbia affords its residents an unusually diverse array of career and lifestyle opportunities. Add a temperate climate and close proximity to both the beach and the mountains, and it's easy to see why George Washington's "uncleared wood" has grown so rapidly into one of the most dynamic cities in the South. ❦

**In the late 1930s, farmers sold and traded goods on Assembly Street in downtown Columbia.** *Courtesy of South Caroliniana Library, University of South Carolina, Columbia*

~ (Above) The former Kress building serves as a symbol of downtown's historic past and its present vitality. *Photo by Suzanne McGrane*

~ (Right) Columbia's wide streets, designed in the 1700s, still provide downtown with a spacious atmosphere. *Photo by Suzanne McGrane*

~ (Below) A fountain on the grounds of the Governor's Mansion offers a quiet spot for sightseers to relax. *Photo by Suzanne McGrane*

# Chapter 3

## Columbia's Finest Treasures

*A wealth of recreational opportunities can be found in
Columbia, including a fun and educational State Museum,
the renowned Riverbanks Zoo and Botanical Garden,
and plenty of places to shop and dine. And for
outdoor pursuits, three nearby rivers provide a scenic getaway.*

☙ **Finlay Park, situated on 18 acres, features a lake and large
playground.** *Photo by Suzanne McGrane*

*Whether you enjoy viewing beautiful strokes that were painted on a canvas more than 100 years ago, smelling the fresh scent of wisteria in the spring, listening to the soft sounds of country music in the park, tasting delicious barbecue, or feeling the warm rays of the Carolina sun during a summer day at the lake, Columbia has something to please every sense and everyone. Its eclectic mix of attractions includes everything from beautiful parks, gardens, and lakes to historic homes, museums, fine dining establishments, and a lively nightlife. The only difficulty in having such a treasure box full of attractions is deciding where to begin.*

Explorers will find art, history, natural history, science, and technology all under one roof at the South Carolina State Museum, located on Gervais Street in downtown Columbia. The museum houses four floors of fascinating exhibits, and even the building itself is an artifact. The South Carolina State Museum is located inside the historic Columbia Mill building, which opened in 1894 as the world's first totally electric textile mill.

The museum is full of other firsts. The science and technology floor houses a life-size replica of the first American-built passenger and freight locomotive, *Best Friend of Charleston*. The museum also showcases the gold Nobel Prize for Physics and a Space Science area that has artifacts from South Carolina's five astronauts, including a rock brought back from the moon. Modern and historic art is showcased in the Lipscomb Art Gallery on the first floor of the museum, and the history floor contains a life-size reproduction of the C.S.S. *Hunley*, the first submarine to sink an enemy ship in combat. In addition, one floor focuses on the history of man, and another is devoted to natural history. Exhibits range from an enormous 43-foot model of the extinct giant white shark to hands-on activities that show how rocks and fossils are formed. With all these opportunities to help make learning fun for kids and parents, it's easy to see why the museum averages between 15,000 and 20,000 visitors a month.

Visitors who enjoy their brush with art in the museum's Lipscomb Art Gallery can browse through several Columbia art galleries on Gervais Street. Then a downtown stroll to the corner of Main and Hampton streets leads to the Columbia Museum of Art, which boasts one of the most impressive collections of Renaissance and Baroque art in the Southeast. The Samuel H. Kress Collection includes works by Botticelli, Tintoretto, Boucher, Canaletto, and others. Additional galleries contain Claude Monet's *L'Ile Aux Orties*;

∾ **An array of intriguing inventions can be found on the Science and Technology floor at South Carolina State Museum.** *Photo by James Quantz Jr.*

🌀 **Tyrannosaurus Rex reigns supreme at the State Museum's dinosaur exhibit.** *Photo by James Quantz Jr.*

🌀 **(Left) McKissick Museum, located on the University of South Carolina campus, has an extensive collection of gemstones, silver, and minerals.** *Photo by Suzanne McGrane*

*Govern*; Evelyn De Morgan's dramatic winged image of Eos; Tiffany glass; and works by regional and national artists and designers such as Frank Lloyd Wright, Paul Wayland Bartlett, J. Scott Goldsmith, Chuck Close, and Robert Rauschenberg.

In addition to its exquisite permanent art collection, the museum offers a variety of traveling art exhibits, preview receptions, adult and children's programs, and concerts. A 7,000-square-foot gallery accommodates the largest traveling exhibitions. Visitors also will find many amenities at the museum, including a cafe area, a children's activity center and art gallery, an art studio, and a 162-seat auditorium for concerts and lectures.

Treasure hunters also will enjoy a trip to the University of South Carolina's McKissick Museum, which includes a priceless collection of beautiful gemstones, silver, and minerals. The McKissick Museum, located on the picturesque Horseshoe in the middle of the USC campus, also tells the tale of university history and houses several permanent and traveling art and science collections.

Youngsters soon will be able to enjoy interactive learning at EdVenture, a world-class, hands-on children's museum.

🌀 **The South Carolina State Museum is located in the old Columbia Mill building on Gervais Street.** *Photo by Suzanne McGrane*

This state-of-the-art museum for the young at heart is scheduled to open in spring 2001. Offering everything from role playing to instruction on musical instruments from the Far East, the museum will provide children with plenty of opportunities to learn while having fun.

Children and adults alike also will delight in the discoveries waiting at Riverbanks Zoo and Botanical Garden, which is one of America's top zoos and among the most popular travel attractions in the Southeast. Home to more than 2,000 animals who thrive in recreated natural habitats with no bars or cages, Riverbanks Zoo offers its own kind of interactive learning. In Riverbanks' 20,000-square-foot birdhouse, visitors enjoy scores of bird songs while watching the endearing penguins dive for food. While on their tour, humans may even experience one of the exhibit's tropical rainstorms. Next, visitors are invited to sample country life at Riverbanks Farm, home of cows, pigs, goats, sheep, rabbits, and chicks. And while there, youngsters and adults can enjoy a cow-milking demonstration. Following a morning on the farm, nothing feels better than a cold splash of water at the sea lion pool. Zoo goers can share some quality time with the sea lions as these graceful creatures swim and frolic.

In the mood for more adventure? Zoo visitors can take a safari to the African Plains and enjoy watching giraffes, zebras, and ostriches in habitats landscaped to reflect the African savannah. Of course, a trip to the zoo would not be complete without a visit to the award-winning 20,000-square-foot Aquarium Reptile Complex, which displays reptiles, amphibians, fish, and invertebrates from around the world. A few steps is all it takes to cross into the desert, which features scaly amphibians, followed by a trek through the tropics, complete with crocodiles. Finally, visitors can end their tour of the complex at the beautiful Indo-Pacific coral reef tank containing sharks, moray eels, and other Pacific Ocean species. And don't forget, a trip to the zoo is never finished without a visit to see the lions, tigers, elephants, monkeys, and polar bears.

can be found during a stroll along the brick paths and in the rose garden. Adding to the scenery are permanent trees, shrubbery, vines, annuals, perennials, and bulbs in every season.

Then visitors can enjoy a stroll through Woodlands Walk and River Trail as they view the naturally landscaped hillside and shoreline. On the trail, visitors will see the ruins of the old Saluda Factory, one of the first water-powered textile mills in South Carolina. Built in 1834, the mill manufactured material used for the Confederate Army's shirts and woolen uniforms.

Intrigued by this glimpse of fascinating history? Columbia's rich heritage is preserved in four historic homes conveniently located downtown—the Hampton-Preston Mansion, the Robert Mills House, the Mann-Simons Cottage, and the Woodrow

**∽ Exquisite plants from all over the world thrive at the Botanical Garden.** *Photo by Suzanne McGrane*

Wilson Boyhood Home. History buffs can peer into the past at these homes, and Christmas candlelight tours and other special events are held throughout the year.

After spending an afternoon with the animals, zoo visitors can walk or ride across a 700-foot bridge over the Saluda River to the dazzling Botanical Garden. Spanning an area larger than a football field, this exquisite garden pleases the senses—from the sweet aroma of daffodils and the lovely array of pinks, purples, and yellows, to the unusual textures of plants from all over the world. A 300-foot canal that features cascades and pinwheel fountains serves as a focal point of the garden. A maze of delightful colors and scents

The Hampton-Preston Mansion was built in 1818 for local merchant Ainsley Hall and was purchased in 1823 by Wade Hampton I. An experienced soldier from the Revolutionary War and a general in the War of 1812, Hampton I was one of the wealthiest landowners in the South. His son and grandson also grew up in the mansion, and his grandson Wade Hampton III went on to become governor of South Carolina. Located on Blanding Street, the home contains Hampton family furnishings and memorabilia dating back to 1810.

The Robert Mills House was designed in 1823 by Robert Mills, the first federal architect of the United States and designer of the Washington Monument, the U.S. Treasury Building, and other notable structures. The home was built for Ainsley Hall, but he died before moving there. The house was bought by the Presbyterian Theological Seminary in 1831 and served this purpose for almost 100 years. Also located on Blanding Street, the Robert Mills House now boasts a Regency decorative arts collection and Regency-style furniture.

The Mann-Simons Cottage was built in 1850 and bought soon afterward by Celia Mann, a former Charleston slave who purchased her freedom with

**∽ A Botanical Garden resident gets ready to make a catch.** *Photo by Suzanne McGrane*

⌒ **A 300-foot canal winds along the Botanical Garden's pathways.**
*Photo by Suzanne McGrane*

money she earned as a midwife. She walked to Columbia and lived in this home on Richland Street as a free black citizen. In 1970 the home was sold to the Columbia Housing Authority. The house features the original dining table and brick fireplace. The ground floor is a gallery where local African-American artists display and sell their works.

The Woodrow Wilson Boyhood Home was built by Woodrow Wilson's parents in 1872, and it was his home during his teenage years. Although he and his parents moved from Columbia in 1875, his parents chose the graveyard of Columbia's First Presbyterian Church as their final resting place. The house, a Victorian structure located on Hampton Street, holds Wilson family memorabilia, original gas lighting fixtures, and the bed where Wilson was born. The garden features magnolias planted by his mother more than 100 years ago. A room in the house depicts the life of Woodrow Wilson, the 28th president of the United States, with pictures and artifacts.

After a stroll through history, sightseers can find many outdoor treasures throughout Columbia. Finlay Park, which was named after a former mayor of Columbia, is the city's most visited park. The 18-acre site features a picturesque waterfall and a cascading stream that spills into the park lake. Outdoor enthusiasts can enjoy a picnic on the lawn, a swing on the playground, or a

game of Frisbee. The park also hosts yearly festivals and events, including a summer concert series. Here, music fans can listen to blues, beach music, reggae, and more while dancing under the stars.

Just down the street from Finlay Park is Riverfront Park and Historic Columbia Canal. Located on Laurel Street, the park is nestled along the banks of the beautiful Congaree River. The canal was used as a source for hydroelectric power, providing electricity in 1895 to the first hydroelectric mill in the world. In 1906 a municipal water plant was built on the canal. Today, in addition to its importance as a source of water and electricity, the canal also offers visitors a unique recreational facility for picnicking, hiking, biking, and jogging. Each spring the park is home to Riverfest, a popular family-oriented festival that features numerous entertainers and exhibitors. Festival proceeds are used to send children with epilepsy to summer camp.

Memorial Park, also in downtown Columbia on Washington Street, pays tribute to the state's veterans. This seven-acre park features a large monument and two free-standing walls with the names of 980 South Carolinians who

More than 2,000 animals make their home at Riverbanks Zoo, which features natural habitats with no bars or cages. Riverbanks ranks among the nation's top 10 zoos. *Photos by Suzanne McGrane*

were killed in Vietnam or are missing in action. There also are memorials for veterans of the China-Burma-India campaigns during World War II and for the U.S.S. *Columbia* CL-56, which was credited for downing 27 planes and assisting in the sinking of two cruisers, two destroyers, and two battleships. A memorial for veterans of the Korean War also is planned.

In addition to these downtown parks, Columbia is home to a 1,440-acre state park. Sesquicentennial State Park, which is 13 miles northeast of downtown Columbia on U.S. Highway 1, is a popular spot for Columbia families. Situated in the Sandhills region, the park offers picnic tables, walking trails, campsites, canoes, and pedal boats.

Outdoor lovers also will enjoy numerous activities on the other side of Columbia at the Midlands' favorite recreational spot—Lake Murray. With 500 miles of shoreline, this man-made, 50,000-acre lake is a paradise for boaters, skiers, swimmers, picnickers, and campers.

In the spring, Lake Murray hosts the Easter Regatta, a prestigious event on the sailing circuit. And, for everyday activities, numerous access areas on the perimeter of the lake are open to the general public. Facilities include boat-launching ramps, picnic shelters, docks, swimming areas, and outdoor grills. There are also commercial boat launch areas and campgrounds around the lake.

After a day at the lake, visitors can experience Columbia's delicious dining and lively nightlife in Five Points. The area draws its name from the five-pronged intersection of Santee Avenue, Harden Street, and Devine Street. By day, Five Points is a trendy shopping district that houses art galleries, unique jewelry and clothing shops, and an array of favorite lunch spots. Every evening a transformation occurs, and Five Points becomes a lively place to enjoy Columbia's nighttime social life.

In Five Points, diners will discover a variety of choices ranging from mouthwatering Italian and tasty Mexican to delicious and familiar American. After their meal, visitors can walk off some calories strolling to one of the area's numerous nightspots. Music lovers can enjoy the riffs of local, regional, and national talents at local bars where Columbia's own Hootie and the Blowfish got its start.

Every Sunday, one pub in Five Points hosts a fun-filled session of Irish music, with as many as 20 performers onstage at a time. It's a weekly warm-up to the exciting St. Paddy's Day Festival, an annual event and Columbia's largest one-day festival. About 100,000 music fans and food lovers gather in the streets at Five Points to celebrate, and the Pot of Gold raised during the event provides more than $100,000 each year to Midlands' not-for-profits. St. Paddy's Day is just one of many festivals celebrated in Columbia; in the

↪ **The Mann-Simons Cottage was owned by Celia Mann, a former slave who purchased her freedom by working as a midwife.** *Photo by Suzanne McGrane*

↪ **(Next page) A walkway in Memorial Park pays tribute to soldiers who defended Pearl Harbor during the infamous World War II attack.** *Photo by Suzanne McGrane*

Midlands, everything from a change of seasons to the delicious taste of fried okra is celebrated.

The three-day Mayfest in Finlay Park attracts more than 150,000 people who enjoy the sounds of live music and culinary delights prepared by local chefs. Autumnfest, held on the grounds of the Hampton-Preston Mansion and Robert Mills House, offers an opportunity to enjoy the arts, play croquet, and taste wines. The Columbia Action Council sponsors the South's largest Veterans Day parade in November and organizes the Carolina Carillon Christmas Parade every December.

The Vista, a renovated commercial district that was formerly empty warehouses, also has become a popular entertainment center. In the fall and spring, Vista Lights and Artista Vista attract thousands to the eclectic mix of galleries, antique shops, restaurants, coffee houses, and nightspots that call the Vista home.

Even more changes are in store for this vibrant, revitalized area. A hands-on children's museum is scheduled to open in Spring 2001, and construction has begun on a riverfront development of homes, nature trails, and restaurants. To read more about this cultural showcase, please turn to page 134.

Not far from the Vista, Columbians can hear the crack of the bat and the roar of the crowd. Professional baseball has had a home in Columbia since 1892, with many teams coming and going through the years. But Bomberball looks as if it is here to stay! The Capital City Bombers began as the Columbia Mets in 1983 and changed their name to the Bombers in

**Boaters can explore more than 500 miles of shoreline on Lake Murray.** *Photo by Suzanne McGrane*

**(Left) Sailing is a favorite pastime on Lake Murray, a 50,000-acre lake located only minutes from downtown Columbia.** *Photo by Suzanne McGrane*

1993. A New York Mets affiliate in the South Atlantic League, the Bombers frequently earn their way into the playoffs and were the 1998 Sally League Champions. Bomber baseball is just another way Columbians can get out and root for the home team.

Also in the spring, the Columbia International Festival celebrates diversity at the State Fairgrounds, where the public is invited to experience the cultures of the world. The festival showcases the sights, sounds, and tastes of dozens of cultures that are part of the Columbia community.

The International Festival highlights the cuisine of many different cultures, but Columbia has a diversity of menus available every day for ethnic food lovers. The region offers several excellent Italian dining establishments that serve authentic, delectable cuisine. A spicy taste of the Far East can be savored at one of many Asian restaurants, with tastes ranging from Szechwan spices to the simplicity of sushi served in traditional formality. Diners can heat up their taste buds with Indian curry or spicy fajitas; an array of tempting feasts is waiting.

An outdoor mural by Columbia artist Lori Truly adds a lively touch to the Filling Station on Devine Street. *Photo by Suzanne McGrane*

(Below) Spectators cheer for a runner during the U.S. Women's Marathon Trials. The event is held in Columbia each February, and winners advance to the U.S. Olympic team. *Photo by Suzanne McGrane*

While Columbia offers these choices and many more, visitors should not depart without a taste of the South. "Real country cooking" can be sampled at local restaurants that serve Southern specialties such as red-eye gravy, collards, okra, red velvet cake, and grits.

Whether visitors choose a stroll through Five Points, sailing on Lake Murray, a concert in Finlay Park, or adventure at the zoo, Columbia contains a wealth of treasures. And no matter what the destination, Columbia always is an exciting place to explore. ◼

**Visitors to Riverbanks Zoo can enjoy a festive light show during the Christmas season.** *Photo by Suzanne McGrane*

~ Every year, more that 100,000 people gather in Five Points for the St. Paddy's Day Festival. Proceeds from the event benefit non-profit agencies in the Columbia area. *Photos by Suzanne McGrane*

~ The annual Oyster Festival attracts thousands of people who enjoy oysters, crawfish, and music on the banks of the Congaree River. *Photo by Suzanne McGrane*

~ (Next page) Maxcy Gregg Park on Blossom Street is a shady spot for a springtime stroll. *Photo by Suzanne McGrane*

Youngsters and adults enjoy a springtime picnic and outing at **Finlay Park.** *Photo by Suzanne McGrane*

# Columbia's Rivers: Untouched Beauty in the Heart of Town

Cutting through the heart of downtown Columbia are not one, but three rivers of incredible purity and beauty—a rare environmental treasure. Here, below the rivers' bluffs and the bustle of downtown, the Saluda and the Broad rivers meet in a frenzy of white rapids, merging to form the tranquil Congaree.

These wonderlands are located only minutes from a thriving metropolitan area, and they offer recreational opportunities usually found in more remote areas. Practically in their back yard, outdoor enthusiasts can enjoy white-water rafting or a relaxing trip by canoe.

### The Lower Saluda River

At the mercy of the Saluda Dam at Lake Murray, the Lower Saluda River flows about 10 miles downstream until it dramatically meets the Broad River. Designated as a State Scenic River by the South Carolina legislature in the early 1990s, the Saluda is a peaceful haven for great blue herons, muskrats, otter, deer, and kingfishers. Drawn from the waters at the bottom of Lake Murray and at a year-round temperature of about 55 degrees, the Saluda's clear, chilly waters are a trout fisherman's dream. In fact, the state's Department of Natural Resources stocks the river regularly with rainbow and brown trout.

Paddlers from all over the country come to experience the thrill of the Lower Saluda's Class II-V white water. Water levels can vary quickly on this river because of the Saluda River Hydro Plant on Lake Murray. South Carolina Electric and Gas Company releases water from the lake based on the demand for power. As a result, the rapids can take paddlers on an exciting ride—or on a downright challenging test of endurance. Rafters should always use caution and call the power company beforehand for information on the water level.

There are two public boat landings on the upper end of the Lower Saluda River—on the south bank of the river off Corley Mill Road and on the other side of the river off Bush River Road. Saluda Shoals Park, a public area off Bush River Road near St. Andrews Road, opened in May 1999. It is a one-of-a-kind park, encompassing a variety of ecosystems and featuring many

∽ **The Lower Saluda River attracts paddlers from all over the country. Water levels and currents can vary widely on the river, so rafters should be prepared to navigate through white-water rapids.**
*Photo by Suzanne McGrane*

opportunities for recreation. The park sits on 270 acres of land, most of it still densely forested. This sparkling section of the Saluda River receives South Carolina's highest water quality rating.

A new, yet-unnamed park currently is under development on the banks of the Saluda. Park planners hope to preserve an important combination of woodlands and wetlands while allowing visitors to enjoy canoeing, kayaking, fishing, nature study, picnics, and hiking. When the park is completed in 2001, it also will feature an outdoor amphitheater, tennis courts, picnic shelters, and meeting and banquet facilities.

### The Broad River

Calm and peaceful before it meets the Saluda, the Broad River is a canoeist's dream. Trees line the banks of the river, hovering and sometimes touching the waters that flow south from the South Carolina piedmont.

➷ **The Broad River's calm waters make it a popular spot for canoeing.** *Photo by Suzanne McGrane*

➷ **(Left) The Saluda River is a haven for birds and many other types of wildlife.** *Photo by Suzanne McGrane*

Paddlers can see flora and fauna of all kinds, including the Rocky Shoals spider lily with its clusters of dark green leaves and white, star-like flowers. This species thrives along the Broad River, but it is rarely seen elsewhere in the world.

The Broad is the least accessible of the rivers flowing through Columbia. Local residents find access points at Harbison State Forest, where some of the best fishing spots along the river are located.

The historic Columbia Canal, originally constructed between 1819 and 1824, helped water freight pass safely around the Broad's shoals and rapids at the confluence. In the late 1890s the canal was reconstructed to be used as a source of hydroelectric power, providing energy to the world's first hydroelectric textile mill.

Today the canal sits beside the municipal water plant and is a backdrop for Riverfront Park, which attracts thousands of people each year. The park features a walking and biking trail that runs for about two miles between the canal and the Broad River. Visitors can enjoy the exquisite beauty of the Broad as it tumbles over rocks and past trees draped with Spanish moss until it joins the Saluda to form the Congaree.

### Congaree River

At the confluence of the Saluda and Broad Rivers, right in the heart of downtown, the Congaree emerges as a calmer river, flowing about 47 miles until it meets the Wateree River. Columbians enjoy the Congaree's more peaceful current for paddling, tubing, boating, and some of the best fishing in the state.

Less than 25 miles downriver from Columbia exists a nature lover's dream—the Congaree Swamp National Monument. To walk the swamp is to be among giants; the area contains some of the tallest trees east of the Mississippi.

**The Congaree River, formed at the confluence of the Broad and Saluda rivers, offers some of the best fishing in the state.** *Photo by Suzanne McGrane*

**(Left) Waters from the Congaree River tumble over the dam at Riverfront Park.** *Photo by Suzanne McGrane*

Here visitors can find plants and animals of all kinds, including approximately 90 tree species and endangered red-cockaded woodpeckers, bobcats, and owls. Visitors are welcome year-round and can see the park by foot or by canoe. Six trails offer more than 18 miles of hiking, and a marked canoe trail on Cedar Creek takes paddlers through beautiful stretches of cypress trees.

Until recently, few people realized the vast potential of Columbia's three rivers. Thanks to individual and group involvement, however, the rivers now play an important role in the area's revitalization.

# Chapter 4

# A Learning Experience

From pre-kindergarten to post-graduate levels, Columbia's educational system excels. During their education and after graduation, students give back to the community in many ways.

⌒⌒ **Columbia College enjoys a reputation as a center for the arts in South Carolina.** *Photo by Suzanne McGrane*

When it comes to excellence in education, Columbia is the place to be—offering award-winning elementary, middle, and high schools; top-ranked private schools; a large university; and single-gender, African-American, and technical colleges. And when students receive an education in Columbia, they also contribute to the community. From entertainment to research and community service, residents reap many benefits from the area's educational institutions.

Education is always a priority among state and city government leaders. That's why there is a never-ending commitment to improve the quality of education in Columbia schools. There are a number of prominent public schools in the Columbia area, and these belong to one of five education districts in Richland and Lexington Counties.

Richland School District One serves the capital city of Columbia and covers 482 square miles. With 51 schools and 27,000 students, this district serves a richly diverse student body that includes children from rural, suburban, and urban areas.

Richland Two is a nationally recognized school district located in suburban northeast Columbia with about 16,600 students and 18 schools. Twelve of these schools have been designated Blue Ribbon Schools by the U.S. Department of Education—testimony to the district's standard of excellence.

Lexington District One is the fastest-growing district in the state, covering 360 square miles and including the towns of Lexington, Gilbert, and Pelion. With 15 schools and an applied technology center that serves its three high schools, Lexington One educates 14,000 students. The district has special programs for advanced placement, at-risk students, and developmentally disabled students as well as remedial programs for 4-year-olds who need extra preparation before they begin school.

Just across the Congaree and Saluda Rivers is Lexington District Two, serving the communities of Cayce, Pine Ridge, South Congaree, Springdale, and West Columbia. This district comprises 15 schools and educates 9,200 students, including 1,316 with disabilities. The district has an Extension Center, a Continuing Education Center, and a transition class located on an Adult Education Campus.

Lexington/Richland School District Five has 10 elementary schools, four middle schools, and four high schools and enrolls more than 14,000 students. This mostly suburban district surrounds the eastern side of Lake Murray and includes the Irmo, Chapin, and Dutch Fork areas of Columbia. District Five led the state for the number of schools with outstanding student performance in the 1997-98 School Incentive Reward Program. These schools were honored for demonstrating outstanding levels of student achievement or for showing significant improvement in student performance between the 1995-96 and 1996-97 school years.

In addition to quality public schools, Columbia also is home to a number of private schools that maintain a strong academic focus. Hammond School teaches boys and girls in preschool through 12th grade. The school boasts

~~ **Eau Claire High School is located in downtown Columbia, where many neighborhoods have undergone a revival in recent years.** *Photo by Suzanne McGrane*

small classes and a talented faculty and is accredited by the National Association for the Education of the Young Child. Heathwood Hall Episcopal School earned the United States Department of Education's National Blue Ribbon Award as a "Recognized School of Excellence." Healthwood is the only college preparatory school in South Carolina to have earned this distinction. Cardinal Newman School, part of the Catholic Diocese of Charleston, is accredited by the Southern Association of Schools and Colleges. Ben Lippen, a Scottish phrase meaning "mountain of trust," is an evangelical Christian school for pre-kindergarten through 12th grade. The school is college preparatory, coeducational and has both boarding and day students. Sloan School prides itself on a progressive learning environment and a challenging curriculum.

The goal of higher education can lead students to one of the most beautiful campuses in America—the University of South Carolina, located on 242 acres in the heart of downtown Columbia. Chartered in 1801 as South Carolina College, the University of South Carolina was the first state university to be supported continuously by annual state appropriations. By mid-century, it had become one of the most distinguished colleges in the United States. The pre-Civil War campus included Longstreet Theatre and all the buildings (with the exception of McKissick Museum) in the area known today as the Horseshoe, a picturesque quadrangle nestled in the center of busy downtown Columbia.

When the voluntary enlistment of all students into the Army of the Confederacy forced the college to close in June 1862, the buildings were used by the Confederate government as a hospital. By the time Sherman's army reached Columbia in February 1865, the hospital housed wounded Union soldiers. Although a fire destroyed most of the city, federal troops helped save campus buildings from the flames.

After reopening in 1865, the institution went through six reorganizations and name changes before the century closed. In 1906, the school was rechartered for the third and final time as the University of South Carolina. Today the University boasts a statewide network of campuses with diverse and inventive education programs.

Named as one of the "Best Values in Higher Education" by *Money* magazine, USC enrolls almost 26,000 students on the Columbia campus, about

∽ **USC's School of Medicine is recognized as a leader in primary care medical education.** *Photo by Suzanne McGrane*

16,000 undergraduates, and about 10,000 in graduate and professional programs. The Columbia campus has more than 1,000 professors who are nationally and internationally known for their teaching, scholarship, and research in the sciences, liberal arts, and professional fields. The University offers more than 350 degree programs, 11 programs of study for associate degrees, master's degrees in 182 areas, and doctorate degrees in 61 areas. Professional doctorates are offered in pharmacy, law, and medicine, and the latter two programs have become increasingly attractive to out-of-state residents.

USC's School of Medicine is recognized as a national leader in primary care medical education. The School of Medicine is one of only seven U.S. medical schools with 50 percent or more of its graduates practicing primary care medicine. The School of Medicine also sponsors research focused primarily on South Carolina health-care needs and furnishes a wide range of clinical care services to South Carolinians.

USC's School of Law was founded in 1866 and has provided thousands of attorneys with a superior legal education. About 750 students are enrolled in the School of Law, located on the USC campus. The percentage of law school graduates who pass the bar exam on the first try each year is among the highest in the Southeast.

◠ The president's home is among the buildings located on the historic Horseshoe, site of USC's original campus. *Photo by Suzanne McGrane*

◠ Splendid architecture is a hallmark of the USC campus. *Photo by Suzanne McGrane*

Many USC programs are nationally and internationally ranked, including geographic information systems, advertising, public relations, school psychology, marketing, marine science, and international business. USC's College of Business Administration repeatedly receives accolades. The International Business Program has continuously ranked as one of the nation's top 10, according to annual surveys by *U.S. News and World Report*. The MIBS program is unique because it prepares students to face challenges in the global business arena.

Another top program at USC is the South Carolina Honors College, which offers academically gifted undergraduates the advantages of a small college education in the context of a large, comprehensive university. Enrollment for the college for 1998-99 was about 900 students, and 85 percent of these were South Carolina residents. *The New York Times* has described the college as a "thriving, undergraduate honors program that operates at Ivy League standards."

The college, as well as the president's residence, are housed on the Horseshoe—site of the university's original campus. A leisurely walk around the Horseshoe is a visit to the past; within four city blocks are 10 buildings from the early 1800s. Listed on the National Register of Historic Places, the buildings have been restored to their original appearance and are used as living quarters, classrooms, and faculty offices.

Robert Mills, the nation's first federal architect and the designer of the Washington Monument, greatly influenced the architecture of these buildings. He was involved in the design of Rutledge College, the South Carolina Library, and Maxcy Monument in the center of the Horseshoe, named for the first president of the college, Jonathon Maxcy.

Maxcy also has a building named after him—Maxcy College—which was built in the 1930s. Over the years, the building has housed students, administrative offices, and a canteen. The college closed in 1996 for extensive renovations, and today the building is home to about 180 Honors College freshmen. A new residential hall, the South Quadrangle, was completed in 1997, providing 100 apartments for 400 upperclassmen. Both of these projects are part of the Bicentennial Campus Master Plan, which aims to preserve the university's historic atmosphere while providing new academic, residence, and campus life facilities. Other projects include the Graduate Research Science Center, and the Strom Thurmond Fitness and Wellness Center.

While the University strives to improve the quality of campus life, students participate in service projects to improve life in their community. The University's 19 fraternities, 13 sororities, 25 service organizations, and many student athletic groups all are committed to helping those in need.

USC students also bring entertainment and the arts to Columbia. USC's Williams-Brice Stadium is a 80,250-seat structure that is home to the Fighting Gamecock football team. With six or seven home games each fall, USC football is nearly a religion in Columbia. Fans enjoy the traditional tailgate feast before each game, and their spirits soar every time the Gamecocks run onto the field to the powerful theme song from *2001*.

The city bursts with excitement for every USC home game. Tailgaters can be found at the State Fairgrounds, the Farmers Market and everywhere in between. New tailgating facilities continue to be built near the stadium to give fans even more venues to celebrate during football season. And with the addition of Lou Holtz in 1999 as head coach of the Gamecocks, football fans are looking to the future with even more enthusiasm.

As soon as football season wraps up, Gamecock fans move indoors to the Carolina Coliseum/Frank McGuire Arena, home to USC's men's and women's basketball teams. Led by Coach Eddie Fogler, the USC men's team draws huge crowds with its action-packed games, and in 2000, the team advanced to the SEC semifinals. The women's basketball team, led by Coach Susan Walvius, plays in the most competitive conference in the country, where the team continues to improve and to excite the crowds. Seating more than 12,000, the Coliseum also attracts musical groups and other events that keep the Columbia community busy throughout the year.

The School of Music entertains more than 20,000 people statewide each year through concerts and music programs. Housed in a beautiful structure, the school is appropriately next door to the equally magnificent Koger Center for the Arts. The center is USC's premier arts facility, showcasing the talents of students, faculty, and community groups, as well as national and international performers. In addition, Longstreet Theatre is a theater-in-the-round that stages numerous University-sponsored performances for the Columbia community.

∽ **Cooper Library serves as a focal point for USC students. Approximately 16,000 undergraduates are enrolled at the school, and 10,000 students are in graduate and professional programs.** *Photo by Suzanne McGrane*

∽ **(Next page) Every fall, thousands of football fans pack Williams-Brice Stadium to watch USC's Fighting Gamecocks.** *Photo by Suzanne McGrane*

Columbia College also enjoys a reputation as a center for the arts in South Carolina. The college offers majors in music, art, and dance. It also sponsors a series of cultural events each year for both students and the community, with events ranging from classical opera to modern dance. A highlight of the cultural events season is the presentation of SoSoHo performances, which brings national talent to the stage of Cottingham Theater.

Founded in 1854 by the South Carolina Methodist Conference "to educate young women for fruitful service to church, state, and nation," Columbia College officially opened in downtown Columbia in 1859 as a private, four-year liberal arts college. The initial enrollment was 188; today 1,200 women attend, and half of these reside on campus. Columbia College is consistently ranked as one of the top 10 liberal arts colleges in the South by *U.S. News and World Report*. It features a 14:1 student/faculty ratio, a campus-wide collaborative learning approach, a nationally recognized honors program, and an emphasis on leadership for women.

Columbia College's honors program is nationally recognized and provides an enriched academic experience for
students who are committed to excellence. The program's
curriculum focuses on a quality liberal arts education,
emphasizing leadership and the lively exchange of ideas in
a challenging classroom environment. The honors program
allows opportunities for independent work on specific
topics, field experiences, and cooperative study at other
institutions around the world.

Columbia is home to two historically African-American
institutions, Benedict College and Allen University, both
located downtown. Benedict College, originally Benedict
Institute, was founded in 1870 to prepare recently emancipated African Americans to meet the challenges ahead.

During its first 25 years, Benedict Institute directed its
educational program to low-income African Americans in
the South. The Institute's original objective was to train
teachers and pastors, and its first curriculum included
reading, writing, spelling, arithmetic, and religion. Later,
the curriculum expanded to include the traditional college

∽ **Columbia College has been located in downtown Columbia
since 1859.** *Photo by Suzanne McGrane*

∽ **(Right) Allen University was founded in 1870 and is one of two
historically African-American colleges in Columbia.** *Photo by Suzanne
McGrane*

Members of the Columbia College faculty are widely recognized as outstanding teachers by educators on the local, regional, and national levels. In addition
to a day program that offers 37 majors, 23 minors, and five preprofessional programs, the college sponsors an independent evening college with majors in
business administration, accounting, public affairs, social work, and entrepreneurship. It also conducts a contractual studies program, which enables academically motivated students to design an individualized curriculum.

Columbia College has earned national distinction for its focus on leadership
studies for women. The college's Leadership Institute perpetuates this mission
by training students to assume leadership positions in their professions and
their communities, and by preparing them to live in a diverse, global society.
The Institute offers leadership programs for women in the community
through lectures, seminars, and workshops. It also provides a forum for
alumnae and other professional women to share experiences and discuss
common issues.

In addition, the college sponsors a Collaborative Learning Center, where
forums are held several times each week. Faculty, staff, students, and community members join in these discussions, and subjects range from "Native
American Spirituality" to "Women in the Legislature." The Center and the
Collaborative Learning program were honored in 1996 with the prestigious
Theodore M. Hesburgh Award, which recognizes faculty efforts to enhance
undergraduate learning.

disciplines and an industrial department offering carpentry, shoemaking,
printing, and painting. Benedict received its college charter in 1894 and
awarded its first bachelor of arts degree that same year.

Under improving economic and social conditions, Benedict has been able
to broaden its objectives and develop a diversified academic program.
Benedict College has been a fully accredited four-year college since 1952.
Today the college enrolls more than 2,000, and it continues to be one of the
nation's premier historically black colleges. Benedict seeks to recruit and
retain quality students, faculty, and staff from various ethnic backgrounds
and geographic areas. Through its varied programs and services, the college
maintains its liberal arts tradition while preparing graduates to meet the
complex demands of today's technological society. Benedict offers a broad
scope of majors in 23 areas of study. The college's curriculum focuses on
careers in business, government, social and health services, public and private
school instruction, the military, and civic, cultural, and scientific work.

Most students live on campus, which provides them with the opportunity
to become involved in athletics, clubs, service organizations, and honor
societies. Benedict strongly encourages students to participate in extracurricular
activities as a tool for self-development. Students also are encouraged to
become involved in arts and humanities because Benedict College believes
this involvement increases the students' appreciation of the arts, enhances
their quality of life, and promotes their interests and talents.

Across the street from Benedict is another historically African-American
college—Allen University. Not only does Allen University share the same
street as Benedict College, it also shares many of the same goals and values.
Allen University is an academic community dedicated to providing baccalaureate
education with a strong commitment to teaching and community service.
Also founded in 1870, this institution represents the dream of Daniel

Alexander Payne, a former slave who become a leading advocate of African-American education. Allen University was named in honor of Richard Allen, founder of the Free African Society and the African Methodist Episcopal Church, who was also a former slave.

Accredited in 1992, the four-year institution offers eight major areas of study. Each program combines theory with practical application, and each also emphasizes personal development, communication skills, and other basic skills students need to be successful in the business world. In addition, students are encouraged to participate in one of several Greek organizations, athletic clubs, and service organizations at Allen University to provide them with a diverse and fulfilling college experience.

Students who want to prepare for four-year schools or who desire a more technical education can find a public trade school, a public technical education center, and a private junior college—all at once—at Midlands Technical College. MTC enrolls about 10,000 students, the state's third-largest undergraduate enrollment. The college employs more than 500 permanent faculty and staff and about 500 adjunct faculty. Each year, faculty members accrue state, regional, and national awards for their superior teaching. MTC offers more than 80 degrees, diplomas, and certificate programs of study. In addition, MTC's continuing education program serves more than 30,000 residents and is one of the largest among two-year colleges in the state.

About one in three college-bound high school graduates in the MTC service area enrolls at Midlands Technical College. MTC is the largest source of transfer students to Columbia College and the University of South Carolina, outside the USC system. MTC also is successful with its students who seek jobs after graduation—95 percent of employers surveyed rated MTC graduates as good or excellent, and more than 98 percent of graduates available for employment during 1996-97 were either employed or continuing their education.

With many K-12 schools and five leading colleges in one town, Columbia provides a variety of educational opportunities for its diverse population. In exchange, students of all ages, races, and backgrounds continue to give back to Columbia through the arts, through community service, and as employees and rising leaders. So whether it's on the field or the stage, in the classroom or in the community, students are making a difference in Columbia. ◪

✎ **Benedict College is one of the nation's premier historically black colleges.** *Photo by Suzanne McGrane*

～ Midlands Technical College enrolls 10,000 students and offers a wide range of educational choices. *Photo by Suzanne McGrane*

# Chapter 5

# An Atmosphere of Creativity

*The Columbia area fosters its artistic community, as a wide range of cultural pursuits proves. With so many opportunities to enjoy local music, art, theater, and dance, fans will find entertaining possibilities every day of the year.*

∽ **Tunnelvision, created by nationally known artist Blue Sky, is located on the AgFirst Farm Credit Bank at the corner of Taylor and Marion streets.** *Photo by Suzanne McGrane*

**When many people think of arts and culture in Columbia, they think of popular culture—specifically of the city's most famous sons, the pop/rock band Hootie and the Blowfish. With one of the biggest-selling debut albums ever, Hootie brought national attention to the Columbia music scene. The band's success turned the spotlight on other local bands as well—particularly when MTV aired a special featuring a dynamic array of young rock bands that keep crowds hopping at Columbia's bars and clubs.**

Columbia is well-known for its contemporary music scene. But those who think of Columbia as a rock'n'roll town might be surprised to learn that it's also a jazz town—and a classical town—and a gospel town—and a bluegrass town. When it comes to music, Columbia offers fans a wide range of choices. And that's the case not just with music, but with all the arts as well. With the state's flagship university located in the heart of the city, it's natural that Columbia would be home to a number of talented painters, dancers, sculptors, writers, actors, and musicians. But what really makes the local arts scene shine is the sense of community that's shared by those who contribute to it, and the support the arts enjoy among the community at large.

Columbia may not be a huge city, but its residents have eclectic cultural tastes—and that inspires a rich diversity of cultural offerings. From philharmonic and jazz quartets to punk bands, from popular musicals and Shakespeare in the Park to avant-garde theater, Columbia's dynamic cultural community really does offer something for everyone.

At the heart of the local arts scene is the Cultural Council of Richland and Lexington Counties. The council serves as an umbrella group whose mission is to promote and provide resources for all kinds of arts organizations in the Midlands. In addition to publishing a bimonthly arts calendar, the Cultural Council works to create partnerships between the arts community and the business community. It also raises money to support artistic endeavors and to enhance the cultural development of the community at large.

∽ (Right) Koger Center, on the University of South Carolina campus, is the area's main venue for theatrical and musical performances. *Photo by Suzanne McGrane*

∽ The South Carolina Philharmonic, which often features internationally acclaimed guest artists, is based in Columbia. *Courtesy of South Carolina Philharmonic*

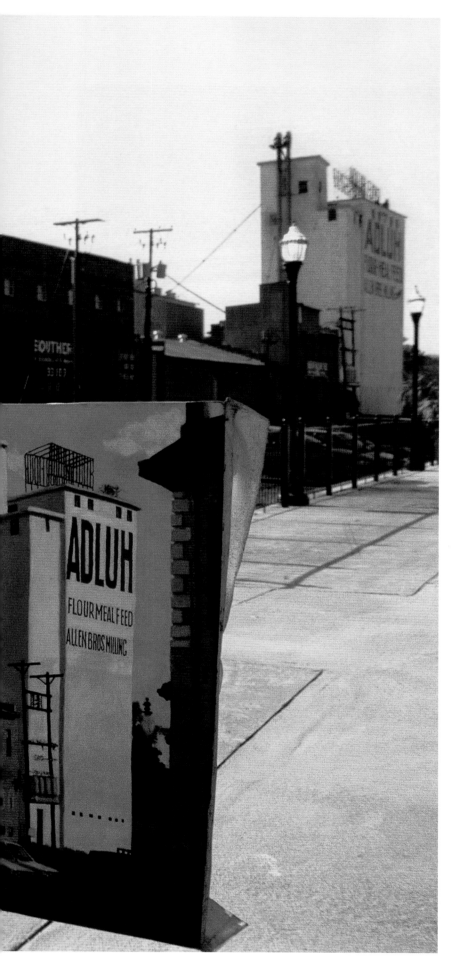

Columbia's artists benefit from the work of the South Carolina Arts Commission as well. Located in Columbia, the South Carolina Arts Commission is one of the strongest and most active state arts commissions in the country. The grants it distributes and the promotional work it performs on behalf of various local visual and performing artists have furthered a number of promising careers.

Many local artists first call Columbia home when they arrive to study in the fine arts or media arts departments at the University of South Carolina. With strong programs in studio art, art education, theater, speech, dance, and music, the university attracts a lot of talent to the Midlands. Many arts students opt to remain in Columbia after graduation because of the supportive environment they find here. Between the university itself, the Arts Commission, the Columbia Museum of Art, and the South Carolina State Museum, Columbia boasts an unusually high number of art institutions for a town its size. As a result, there are many opportunities for artists to show their work and to find employment as teachers. Networks between artists, both formal and informal, further strengthen Columbia's artistic community. Groups of visual artists such as Cats on a Leash work together to stage shows and exhibitions, while organizations such as the Columbia Design League provide a forum for discussion of the future of the visual arts in Columbia.

Many visual artists make their home in Columbia—not only painters but also muralists, photographers, sculptors, printmakers, and potters. Among this group are nationally known artists such as Lee Malerich and Blue Sky. And although neither was a lifelong resident, Jasper Johns lived here while studying at the University of South Carolina, and Georgia O'Keefe taught at Columbia College.

Over the years, many of the city's visual artists have set up shop in the Congaree Vista—a once-neglected area that now supports a thriving community of studios, galleries, and nightspots. But while it's certainly a perfect artistic environment, the Vista is far from the only place to see local works on display. More than 40 art galleries are scattered all over town—a number that attests to the artistic appreciation of Columbia's residents. Groups also sponsor local exhibits in public places throughout the city. These projects include the City Arts Series at Bank of America Plaza, a partnership between the arts and business communities.

Locally produced artwork also can be found at area museums. The South Carolina State Museum, the McKissick Museum, and the Columbia Museum of Art regularly display works by local talents; in fact, many of these items are included in their permanent collections. These museums are also a great resource for artists and art lovers alike. The McKissick Museum has a particularly extensive collection of Southern folk art. The Columbia Museum of Art is home to one of the Southeast's most impressive collections of Baroque and Renaissance paintings, sculpture, and furniture. Both museums also sponsor lectures, concerts, and other arts-related events.

**Columbia artist William Waite paints a landscape of the Adluh Flour Company in the Congaree Vista.** *Photo by Suzanne McGrane*

〜 **The Columbia City Ballet's production of "Dracula: Ballet with a Bite" stars William Starrett, center, as Count Dracula.** *Photo by Allen Anderson*

If Columbians enjoy the visual arts, they are perhaps even bigger fans of the performing arts. One of the most enduring arts traditions in town is dance. The Columbia City Ballet (CCB), South Carolina's oldest dance company, was founded in 1961 and has developed into a professional ballet company with a national impact. The CCB draws dancers from all over the country—and from around the globe—to Columbia, delighting local audiences with performances of traditional classics such as *The Nutcracker* and *Swan Lake*, as well as avant-garde works such as *The Rites of Spring*. CCB also has become known for premiering original works created by its artistic director, William Starrett. Among these are the perennially popular *Dracula* and the critically acclaimed *Don Juan*. And CCB isn't the only ballet in town. Both the Carolina Ballet and the Columbia Classical Ballet Company also

stage a full range of productions each year, and the SouthEast Center for Dance Education, a unique partnership between the Department of Education, the Arts Commission, and several local colleges, brings dance education into area schools, serving students in grades K-12.

Perhaps more than anything else, Columbia is known for its dramatic arts. An impressive number of thriving local theaters is testimony to how much Columbians like to be entertained by a good show. Longstanding mainstays of the Columbia theater scene include Workshop Theatre, Chapin Community Theatre, and the Lexington County Arts Association at the Village Square Theatre in Lexington. But none of these is as old as Town Theatre, which was established in 1919 and is the oldest continuously operating community theater in America. Then there's Trustus Theatre, a professional theater that has earned Constituency Theatre status from the Theatre Communications Group—establishing its place among the top regional theaters in the country. Trustus is the place to go for popular late-night shows on the weekends—with selections ranging from light-hearted farce to provocative drama—and for excellently staged productions of critically acclaimed plays. Whether it's an edgy modern drama at Trustus, a witty comedy at Workshop, or a classic musical at Town Theatre, it's not uncommon for stage productions in Columbia to sell out, so savvy theater-goers know to reserve tickets early. Fortunately, popular shows often are held over or reprised.

One of Columbia's most popular theatrical traditions doesn't even take place in a theater. As its name suggests, Shakespeare in the Park stages productions outdoors, and performances typically draw both large crowds and enthusiastic reviews. Also well attended are plays at local colleges. The University of South Carolina, Columbia College, and Benedict College all have active theater departments. Theater aficionados shouldn't miss the chance to catch a play at USC's Longstreet Theatre, which is not only one of the oldest buildings on campus but also has a round stage. And fans of improvisational comedy can get their funny bones tickled by the We're Not Your Mother Players, who perform regularly at the Art Bar, located in the Vista.

In case local productions aren't enough, touring companies regularly pass through town, too, staging Broadway shows and other popular favorites at USC's Koger Center or the Township Auditorium. Whether your taste runs to Greek tragedy, Restoration comedy, popular musicals, cutting-edge drama, or anything in between, you're sure to have plenty of theatergoing options in Columbia.

Then there's Columbia's most unique contribution to the dramatic arts—the Columbia Marionette Theatre. One of just 20 marionette theaters in the United States, the Columbia Marionette Theatre is the only building in the country that was constructed solely for the purpose of marionette performances. The company tours all over the state, but every weekend its members return to their Laurel Street theater. Here, the group delights youngsters and adults alike with masterful puppetry and witty stories.

**Exhibits at the Columbia Museum of Art include ornate glass chandeliers, above, and an extensive collection of Baroque and Renaissance artwork, below.** *Photos by Suzanne McGrane*

Columbia's involvement with the dramatic arts doesn't end with live theater. Thanks to the efforts of the South Carolina Film Commission, the Palmetto State has been "discovered" by Hollywood as a great place to make movies. South Carolina's warm climate and varied topography have been attracting filmmakers in droves for the past decade, and Columbia has garnered its share of this cinematographic attention. The popular feature films *Renaissance Man* and *The Program* were both filmed largely in Columbia.

Love of the cinematic arts has prompted the founding of the Columbia Film Society and the Creative Music and Film Society, which both screen independent and foreign films. The Columbia Film Society makes its home at the Nickelodeon Theatre on Main Street, which is a stop on the Southern Circuit Filmmakers Tour. The Creative Music and Film Society shows movies every week at USC's Gambrell Hall Auditorium.

As its name suggests, the Creative Music and Film Society is also a forum for music

lovers—specifically jazz lovers. The jazz scene in Columbia is not large, but it is vital. Groups such as the Terry Rosen Quartet and Third Eye Lounge draw enthusiastic crowds every time they play. And jazz is just one type of music that's performed live in Columbia every week. Fans of Celtic music can gather at the Publick House every Sunday for a big celebration. Local rock bands perform throughout the week at popular nightspots such as the New Brookland Tavern, the Art Bar, and the Elbow Room, which also books rock, alternative, and country bands from all over the country. Live country music can be found at West Columbia venues such as the Skyline Club.

Big-name acts such as Reba McEntire, Paul McCartney, Elton John, and Bruce Springsteen pass through town fairly frequently, too, playing at the Carolina Coliseum, the Township Auditorium, or Williams-Brice Stadium, which was the site of the 1996 Farm Aid concert.

∽ **Above, children talk to one of the "actors" while taking a backstage tour of the Marionette Theatre. Below, the company stages a production of "The Wizard of Oz."** *Photos by Suzanne McGrane*

Just as vibrant as Columbia's popular music scene is its classical music scene. The South Carolina Philharmonic, a professional orchestra that routinely features internationally renowned guest artists, is based in town and performs at USC's Koger Center. Popular programs include Saturday

Symphonies, Friday Classics, and Philharmonic Pops. The USC Symphony Orchestra, made up of talented student performers, also attracts enthusiastic crowds, as do chamber music groups such as the Carolina Chamber Players and the Sterling Chamber Players. Choral groups abound here, too. Many are based at local churches and perform within a range of religious traditions from gospel to anthems and cantatas.

Columbia's active live music scene is complemented by the programming of its radio stations. Both the local college radio station, WUSC, and the local National Public Radio station devote specialty programs to jazz, folk, and blues. In fact, Columbia's National Public Radio station is the home of the nationally syndicated Marian McPartland's Piano Jazz. And its sister television station, SCETV, is one of the most prominent public television stations in the country. SCETV produces several nationally popular programs, among them *Nature Scene* and *Firing Line*.

Columbia is also home to a variety of writers. Acclaimed poet and novelist James Dickey lived here and taught at the University for many years. Other local authors of note include popular humorist William Price Fox and novelist Sara Gilbert. A strong creative writing program at USC and a number of local writers' groups develop and nurture new talent. The Art Bar provides a perfect forum for these writers with a weekly open mike program called Two Worlds Collide.

∽ **Every weekend, the puppets' antics delight audiences at the Marionette Theatre.** *Photo by Suzanne McGrane*

∽ **(Next page) Eric Lake's mural on Park Street traces the history of Columbia.** *Photo by Suzanne McGrane*

All this artistic activity around town makes it no surprise that Columbia's cultural calendar is chock full of popular events. With so many offerings, there are bound to be times when culture lovers face two or more tough choices. But that, as Columbia residents will tell you, is a small price to pay for living in such a vibrantly creative community. ◖

CIVIL WAR

# Chapter 6

# A Place to Call Home

*Columbia's homes range from palatial mansions to cozy bungalows, and every style in between. Such an eclectic mix of neighborhoods means that residents can always find a home to perfectly suit their lifestyle.*

*Photo by Suzanne McGrane*

A fast-growing area with a long history, Columbia is home to an impressively eclectic array of residential neighborhoods. Columbians can live in Victorian splendor in downtown neighborhoods like Elmwood Park, they can opt for the comfort and ease of a new house in a modern suburb, or they can find almost anything in between. New or old, each of Columbia's neighborhoods has a distinctive flavor all its own.

### Downtown

Take a walk down the quiet, tree-lined streets of Elmwood Park, and it's hard to believe that Columbia's downtown commercial district is just blocks away. Elmwood Park's central location is just one reason why it ranks among Columbia's most desirable neighborhoods. Characterized by spacious Victorian houses with wide front porches and deep yards, Elmwood Park is the oldest exclusively residential neighborhood in town. Built long before the advent of central air-conditioning, its homes feature lots of windows, beautiful hardwood floors, and ornate fixtures. Spacious, high-ceilinged rooms not only provide welcome relief from hot summer weather but also allow for gracious, comfortable living year-round.

Also enjoying a renaissance of late are many of Columbia's other downtown neighborhoods—among them Cottontown, Earlwood, Eau Claire, and Olympia.

Adjacent to Elmwood Park, Cottontown and Earlwood are characterized by the same quiet, shaded streets but feature smaller, bungalow-style homes dating from the 1930s and '40s. Sprawling north from downtown, Eau Claire was Columbia's first suburb and is known today as one of the city's most eclectic and dynamic communities. Originally built as a mill village on the edge of town, Olympia has a distinct look that is not found anywhere else in Columbia. Its saltbox-style houses and wood-frame duplexes almost give it the flavor of a New England community, and its proximity to the University of South Carolina makes Olympia a popular neighborhood among students who live off campus.

New homes also are available downtown, most notably in the attractive Governor's Hill community, which features elegant town homes with spectacular views of Finlay Park and the city skyline. And upscale loft apartments in the Congaree Vista have become a popular choice among artists and young professionals.

### Five Points/Shandon

Once considered suburbs but now regarded as offering the best in-city living, neighborhoods like Shandon, Wales Garden, Melrose Heights, and Rosewood grew up around the Five Points commercial district in the early decades of the 20th century. Featuring a wide variety of architectural styles, these neighborhoods are best known for the cozy brick and wood-frame

**Homes with a Victorian flair can be found on Park Street in the Elmwood Park area.** *Photo by Suzanne McGrane*

bungalows that are often referred to as "Shandon-style" homes. But no particular design really predominates in these neighborhoods; indeed, it is not uncommon to find small duplexes nestled next to imposing estate-style homes. The diversity of housing options makes these communities socially diverse as well; in addition to being the neighborhoods of choice for many prominent local citizens, they are heavily populated by college students, retirees, and young families. Wide, tree-lined streets make Shandon in particular a mecca for joggers, cyclists, and walkers, and each of these neighborhoods features at least one community park that offers activities for residents of all ages. With suburban-style spaciousness and quiet combined with the proximity to downtown and the university, it's easy to see why these neighborhoods offer "the best of both worlds."

### Heathwood/Lake Katherine

When spring comes to Heathwood, this subtly upscale neighborhood's streets and sidewalks become filled with pedestrians who want to experience Columbia at its most beautiful. First developed in the 1920s, Heathwood features some of the city's most impressive homes and gardens. And like

✑ **The neighborhood of Heathwood, first developed in the 1920s, features a wide variety of architectural styles.** *Photo by Suzanne McGrane*

most in-town neighborhoods, Heathwood's architecture is diverse, encompassing everything from spacious brick colonials to cozy cottages to sprawling ranch-style homes. Big yards and winding streets add to its charm, making Heathwood a premier example of gracious Southern living.

Just to the east is Lake Katherine, one of Columbia's newer and larger in-town neighborhoods. Dating primarily from the 1950s to the 1980s, the homes of Lake Katherine are clustered around a series of lakes that gives the community an atmosphere of expansive serenity. Spacious modern homes, excellent schools, and proximity to both downtown and the Columbia beltway have made Lake Katherine a particularly popular choice among young families.

### Southeast

Columbia is a fast-growing city, but its excellent highway system still makes it possible for residents to live in a rural setting without having to

∽ **Azaleas and dogwood blooms add charm to a home in Laurel Hill.** *Photo by Suzanne McGrane*

make an arduous commute into town. Among those who work in Columbia but prefer to make their homes outside the city, one of the most desirable places to live is in the rolling farmland that stretches to the south and east along Highway 378. This is horse country, where split-rail fences wind lazily through fields that surround elegant manor houses and contemporary ranch houses. It's also the site for housing developments that offer residents the dual conveniences of an easy commute and a country retreat complete with popular amenities like tennis and swimming.

Closer to town, the southeastern corridor is surrounded by several large residential neighborhoods that are convenient to Fort Jackson and to downtown Columbia. While this area was well-established by the 1970s, new development is still taking place in east Columbia, making it one of the closest and most affordable sites for a new home. In addition to smaller starter homes, east Columbia's residential neighborhoods offer many choices ranging from comfortable ranches and trilevels to elegant mansions.

### Northeast Columbia

Someone looking for all the social pleasures of quiet suburban living and the convenience of a 15-minute drive from downtown will find the perfect neighborhood in northeast Columbia. This area features some of the finest newer neighborhoods in the Columbia suburbs, award-winning schools, and numerous well-maintained golf courses and country clubs.

Premier new home communities boast amenities for every lifestyle including

∽ **Many students live in the area around Greene Street, which is close to USC.** *Photo by Suzanne McGrane*

tennis, walking trails, playgrounds, swimming, golf, and fishing—often right within the development's perimeter. Neighborhoods are intimate and inviting; neighbors often greet each other while pushing strollers, jogging, or walking on tree-lined streets and sidewalks. Residents of this area also enjoy participating in activities of the Northeast Columbia Association, an organization designed to bring the neighbors of the northeast together for fun and relaxation.

Northeast Columbia residents have easy access to shopping at Columbia Mall and numerous retail stores. Restaurants abound, and northeast residents need not travel downtown for a delicious meal. For picnickers, hikers, and nature lovers, Sesquicentennial State Park is located right in the heart of this growing area.

### Northwest Columbia

Northwest Columbia boasts some of the area's most scenic residential sites. This region, which includes St. Andrews, the towns of Irmo and Lexington, booming Harbison, and beautiful Lake Murray, is one of the fastest-growing in the Midlands. As builders construct new houses in expanding developments, the shopping and amenities in the northwest have grown in proportion, too. Residents enjoy the close proximity to downtown Columbia, a wide variety of beautiful housing communities, and convenience to quality stores and shops, including Columbiana and Dutch Square malls.

This area also features a wealth of recreational assets. Lake Murray Dam is nearby with both a boat access and public swimming area. People can go white-water rafting or canoeing on the Lower Saluda River, which runs right through this region. Harbison State Forest also offers outdoor enthusiasts plenty of options such as hiking, biking, fishing, and exploring nature.

For those who would like to enjoy the Carolina sunset over sparkling blue water right in their backyard, there's Lake Murray. This large lake has more than 550 miles of shoreline and while Lake Murray's original function was to supply electric power, it has become the water playground for the Midlands and a choice location for many homes. Living on Lake Murray means access to adventure; boating, picnicking, fishing, water skiing, and swimming are just a few popular pastimes.

For those who don't live right on the lake, South Carolina Electric and Gas Company provides numerous public access areas on the perimeter of the lake. Facilities include boat-launching ramps, picnic shelters, docks, swimming, outdoor grills, and restrooms. In addition, there are numerous commercial boat launch areas and campgrounds around the lake.

### Forest Acres/Arcadia Lakes

Next to the Columbia city limits lies the City of Forest Acres and the Town of Arcadia Lakes. This community of tall pine trees and quiet streets provides people both young and old with the best of suburban living.

꩜ **Shandon, located near Five Points, is a popular neighborhood for families with younger children.** *Photo by Suzanne McGrane*

Residents have access to some of the state's best schools, and neighborhoods boast distinctive, well-maintained brick homes.

Many of the neighborhoods in this area lie near a stream called Gills Creek. This watershed has been dammed in numerous places, creating beautiful ponds and lakes around the community. Many residents enjoy backyard access to these waterways, which provide opportunities for fishing, boating, and swimming.

Residents of Forest Acres and Arcadia Lakes enjoy the convenience of major shopping malls, including Richland Fashion Mall and Columbia Mall. Movie theaters, grocery stores, and specialty shops also are only a short drive from these quaint neighborhoods. Interstate 77 and 20 are nearby, so whether Columbians work at Fort Jackson, downtown or out of town, traveling to and from home is easy.

The small communities that lie beyond the city's border have small-town charm and the conveniences of city living. The towns of Lake Elizabeth, Denny Terrace, and Cedar Creek are located in eastern Richland County. Southern Lexington County has Gaston, Swansea, and Pelion. And in western Lexington County are the towns of Batesburg, Leesville, and Gilbert.

Urban, suburban, rural—Columbia's wealth of different housing possibilities ensures that there's something for everyone in the Midlands. Newcomers marvel at the affordability of housing in the Columbia area; the average price was $118,906 in 1998. And no matter where they live, all Columbians enjoy the convenience of easy access to great restaurants, malls, schools, and recreational facilities. No wonder Columbia's been growing so fast; once they've had a taste of the lifestyle, few people want to leave! ◗

〜 **Lake Murray, in scenic northwest Columbia, is a choice location for upscale homes.** *Photo by Suzanne McGrane*

∾ Springtime in Columbia brings an array of festive blooms.
*Photos by Suzanne McGrane*

# Chapter 7

# *Lending a Helping Hand*

Through churches, non-profit agencies and businesses, caring
Columbians volunteer their time and contribute generously
to help those in need. And in addition, outstanding hospitals
offer another level of care that benefits the entire area.

⌒ **Spring flowers add a colorful touch to Trenholm Road Methodist
Church.** *Photo by Suzanne McGrane*

*Spring, summer, winter, or fall—it's always the season for giving in Columbia. Altruistic Columbians can be found throughout the area—in churches, shelters, specialty homes, businesses, and hospitals. Columbia's helping hands reach far and wide—and touch both hearts and souls.*

Columbia is a city enriched by many historic churches, and most are located downtown. The oldest churches date back to the 1830s and include First Baptist Church, Ladson Presbyterian Church, and St. Peter's Catholic Church. Other churches such as Ebenezer Lutheran Church and Washington Street United Methodist Church were rebuilt after Sherman's troops burned Columbia in 1865. Another historic church, Trinity Episcopal Cathedral, is a replica of York Minster Cathedral in England. Trinity Episcopal is listed on the National Register of Historic Places and has six former state governors buried in its graveyard.

Columbia's Jewish community also traces its roots back to the 1800s. German Jewish settlers built a synagogue, and it was rebuilt after being destroyed by Sherman's troops. Today, outreach efforts are conducted through the Jewish Community Center and the conservative, egalitarian Beth Shalom Synagogue, which now has the largest membership in its history.

Many new churches also offer services and special programs for youth, singles, young married couples, families, and senior adults. There are more than 60 Protestant churches along with a number of large Roman Catholic and Greek Orthodox churches. In addition, there are communities of Baha'is, Buddhists, Hindus, Muslims, and Mormons. No matter what the faith, visitors are always welcome to join worship services.

Generosity is a common message at these churches, synagogues, and temples, so it's no surprise that these same religious institutions are very active in Columbia's community service. Holding clothing and food drives for the needy, collecting money for families in crisis, and providing shelter for the homeless are just a few ways that churches make a difference in the lives of those less fortunate. Another way religious institutions help the community is by partnering with Columbia's non-profit agencies, whose mission is to better the lives of people in need.

ᴄᴚᴐ **Founded in 1964, the recently renovated Kathwood Baptist Church makes a difference in the Forest Acres neighborhood.** *Photo by Suzanne McGrane*

Columbia not-for-profits offer family support and crisis intervention; aid for children and at-risk youth; care for older residents; help for the homeless and hungry; assistance for children and adults with illnesses; services for people with physical, mental, and developmental disabilities; literacy education; emergency assistance; and shelter and aid to abused women and children. And in an effort to offer assistance and compassion to everyone who needs it, Columbia not-for-profits count on the community to donate both time and money.

The United Way and area college community service programs serve the Columbia area with much-needed resources. City Year Columbia serves as another community link to the not-for-profit sector. City Year operates in only 11 sites around the country and serves to connect young adults to their communities. Part of the national service entity AmeriCorps, City Year is built on the Rev. Dr. Martin Luther King Jr.'s idea of a "beloved community"— a place where justice and peace prevail.

City Year Columbia was founded in 1993. Young Columbians ages 17-24 participate in City Year for 10 months, developing leadership and citizenship skills while performing community service and earning money for college. Members receive social training in serving children, and in painting, land-scaping, and carpentry. To graduate from the program, participants must perform

  Bethel AME Church is on Woodrow Street at the former site of Shandon Baptist Church. Bethel AME was founded in 1866. *Photo by Suzanne McGrane*

1,700 hours of service. City Year members tutor and mentor elementary schoolchildren, turn vacant lots into gardens and playgrounds, teach young-sters about the dangers of drug and alcohol abuse, build walking trails at parks and schools, renovate low-income housing, and provide in-home assis-tance to elderly residents of city housing units.

City Year Columbia also encourages all citizens to join its annual Serve-A-Thon in mid-October. The day-long event attracts thousands of Columbians who lend their time and talents to work on City Year projects. Residents also show their community support by participating in charity walks that are held throughout the year. Some of Columbia's more popular walks include Palmetto Health Alliance's First Ladies' Walk for Life: Steps Against Breast Cancer, the March of Dimes' WalkAmerica, the Juvenile Diabetes' Walk to Cure Diabetes, Common Threads' AIDSWalk, and the American Cancer Society's Relay for Life.

Columbia companies also make it their business to give back to the community. These firms encourage employee participation in charitable events, and they also generously support the area's not-for-profits, providing

sponsorship dollars, in-kind services such as office space and printing materials, and promotional assistance. This dedication to community service is recognized through the mayor's Corporate Citizen of the Year Award. The award goes to a Columbia business that has shown strong leadership, a dedication to community service, and a commitment to overall citizenship.

One program that benefits from corporate sponsorship is First Steps, which is aimed at improving early childhood development. First Steps provides support for families to ensure their children are prepared to enter first grade. Through the program, youngsters start school with the skills they need to succeed.

Residents and businesses alike are reaching out to Columbia's less fortunate in many ways. From Sistercare and Meals on Wheels to the Columbia City Ballet and the Columbia Museum of Art, nonprofit agencies are enjoying both monetary support and helping hands from thousands of Columbians.

Serving the community also is the mission of the area's three full-time health-care providers—Palmetto Health Alliance, Providence Hospital, and Lexington Medical Center.

Richland Memorial Hospital and Baptist Medical Center, two long-standing, leading hospitals in the Midlands, joined forces in February 1998 to become the Palmetto Health Alliance. This new system also

**Lexington Medical Center attracts some of the region's leading health-care professionals.** *Photo by Suzanne McGrane*

**(Right) Devine Street is home to Shandon United Methodist Church.** *Photo by Suzanne McGrane*

includes a hospital in the upstate—Palmetto Baptist Center-Easley. The Alliance aims to bring significant financial savings and enhanced benefits to the community, including greater access to care under a locally controlled health-care system.

Palmetto Richland Memorial Hospital has been serving patients in the Columbia area for more than 100 years. The facility provides a center for specialty services, including the only partially matched bone marrow transplantation program in South Carolina and the only Level 1 trauma center in the Midlands. Other areas of expertise include high-risk obstetrics, orthopaedics, psychiatry, cardiology, oncology, nephrology, neonatology, neurology, neurosurgery, and medical/surgical services. In 1997, the Bone Marrow Transplant division was chosen as one of 12 test sites in the United

SHANDON UNITED METHODIST CHURCH

States to participate in clinical trials for patients undergoing high-dose chemotherapy and stem cell transplants. And the Kidney Transplant program at Palmetto Richland is one of only two such programs in the state.

Palmetto Baptist Medical Center was founded in 1914. Although its name has changed, its mission remains the same—providing high-quality, cost-efficient health care for the Columbia community. Palmetto Baptist has earned a reputation as one of the finest hospitals in the Southeast, with areas of excellence including oncology, behavioral health, orthopaedics, and women's and children's services. Readers of *The State*, South Carolina's largest daily newspaper, have named Palmetto the "Best Hospital" for nine consecutive years. In addition to its local services, about 12,000 upstate residents are served annually by Palmetto Baptist-Easley's off-campus Community Education Center, which provides free blood pressure screenings and a variety of health classes.

Palmetto Health Alliance also has collaborated with other institutions to serve the community at large. In 1999, the Alliance and the University of South Carolina School of Medicine created the South Carolina Cancer Center. The SCCC is one of the largest comprehensive cancer programs in the Southeast, and it focuses on education, prevention, early detection, treatment, and supporting the needs of patients and families.

Another Columbia hospital that is committed to providing outstanding care to the community is Providence Hospital, operated by the Sisters of Charity of St. Augustine. An acute-care, 247-bed facility, Providence

✑ **Providence Hospital has earned designation as a Center for Excellence for its work preventing, diagnosing, and treating cardiovascular disease.** *Photo by Suzanne McGrane*

✑ **(Right) Richland Memorial Hospital and Baptist Medical Center have joined forces to become Palmetto Health Alliance.** *Photo by Suzanne McGrane*

often is called the "Heart Hospital" because it is a nationally known Center of Excellence for the prevention, diagnosis, and treatment of cardiovascular disease.

Providence Heart Institute, equipped with five catheterization labs, four surgical suites, and an electrophysiology lab, is consistently among the first to introduce advances in heart surgery procedures. The institute is ranked among the nation's premier heart centers, and more than 6,000 procedures are conducted there annually.

However, repairing broken hearts isn't all Providence does. As a recognized leader in the fields of ophthalmology and general surgery, Providence Hospital Eye Surgery Center is the setting for the most advanced technology in laser eye surgery, and excellent care is provided by the Outpatient Surgery Center. Additional services include internal and family medicine, gastroenterology, endoscopy lab services, sleep studies, orthopaedics, otolaryngology, physical rehabilitation, diabetes care services, and emergency care.

The annual Group Therapy Chili Cookoff spices up life in Columbia. Group Therapy, a popular bar in Five Points, sponsors the event and proceeds benefit The Babcock Center, a facility for the mentally and physically disabled. Thousands of people—and even a few lucky pets—crowd the streets downtown to sample chili chefs' creations. *Photos by Suzanne McGrane*

Opened in March 1999, Providence Hospital Northeast serves the needs of northeastern Richland County. As a community hospital licensed for 46 acute care and 18 skilled subacute care beds, Providence Northeast focuses on family medicine and offers diagnostic services, emergency care, medical/surgical services, maternity care, and transitional care.

Providence is also a source of health education for the Midlands area. The goal of its Community Health Services department is to provide vital information to residents through a variety of classes and services. Programs include diabetes education, driving instruction for seniors, weight management, CPR courses, support groups, and special health screenings.

In Lexington County, Lexington Medical Center offers state-of-the-art facilities and attracts some of the region's leading health-care professionals. When it opened in 1971, Lexington Medical Center promised to treat its patients as individuals and to provide the special services necessary for their complete care—commitments that continue today. For example, in maternity services, Lexington Medical Center was first to offer birthing suites and first to invite fathers to participate in the birthing experience. Lexington Medical Center also was the first area hospital to feature midwives and doulas, non-clinical staff people who assist parents during delivery.

In addition to its large nursery, Lexington Medical Center's 20-bassinet Special Care nursery provides for the most fragile newborns. Another first, Lexington Medical Center's Kangaroo Care program, helps mothers bond with their premature infants and encourages faster recoveries. To help parents answer the many questions that arise once they return home with their bundles of joy, Lexington Medical Center provides a free educational video at discharge, plus a 24-hour direct line to its nurses.

∽ **Volunteers in the United Way Leadersteps program work on the grounds at Arthurtown Community Center. The center holds child development programs for infants and children up to age 4. It also conducts after-school programs for youngsters in elementary school.**
*Photo by Suzanne McGrane*

While Lexington Medical Center welcomes its patients, its ultimate goal is to help Columbians avoid a hospital stay altogether. Therefore, for more than 28 years, Lexington Medical Center has been a leader in health education. It sponsors health fairs and on-site health programs for companies and trade shows—all emphasizing the importance of early detection when combating illness. To stress this message, Lexington offers free services at these events such as screenings for cholesterol, blood sugar, and diseases such as cancer.

Through its Health Directions Program, Lexington Medical Center also provides a complete array of health and wellness classes such as aerobics, weight management, infant care, and healthy cooking, plus ongoing seminars on topics such as smoking cessation and menopause.

Columbia area churches, nonprofit agencies, and health-care providers share common commitments—to offer help and hope to those in need. With remarkable dedication and unity of spirit, caring Columbians are continuing their city's tradition of gracious Southern hospitality. ⊡

~ (Above) Patients in the cancer treatment program at Palmetto Richland Memorial Hospital can stay with their families at Caring House. The home offers comfortable accommodations and is conveniently located on the hospital grounds. *Photo by Suzanne McGrane*

~ (Below) The Wine Tasting Silent Auction, held by the SOS Foundation, helps cancer patients in the Richland Memorial Bone Marrow Transplant program. When the event was held in February 2000, generous donations by local artists, restaurant owners, wine distributors, and food distributors helped to raise $10,000. *Photo by Suzanne McGrane*

ᗡᖇ (Above) The South Carolina Cancer Center's Healing Garden, for patients and their families, is on the grounds of the center next to Palmetto Richland Memorial Hospital. *Photo by Suzanne McGrane*

ᗡᖇ (Below) Every October, thousands of participants join the Palmetto Health Alliance Walk for Life, which raises money to treat breast cancer. *Photo by Suzanne McGrane*

Camp Kemo brings summer fun to youngsters who are undergoing chemotherapy or are former chemotherapy patients. The facility is run by volunteers, and doctors and nurses are on staff to provide care. Campers take part in a variety of outdoor activities including swimming and trail rides. *Photos by Suzanne McGrane*

# Chapter 8

# Into the 21<sup>st</sup> Century

*As the new century begins, Columbia is enjoying prosperity and is poised for more economic success. Through development and revitalization projects, Columbians are steadily building for the future.*

◌ **Preserving Columbia's rivers is a major focus of the city's plans for the new century.** *Photo by Suzanne McGrane*

Columbia's time has arrived. As the city enters the 21st century, it is fast becoming one of the nation's premier communities to live in and to visit. Columbia's tremendous transformation from an average city to one of the most dynamic areas in the South did not happen overnight. It is a result of years of careful planning and prudent implementation of proposals designed to boost business and create an atmosphere that attracts people to the metropolitan area.

What makes Columbia's vision for the future an extraordinary venture— one vastly different from plans of other communities? It is because this revitalization effort encompasses the dreams, desires, and heart of community leaders and citizens throughout the area. The cooperation achieved to create Columbia's renaissance is truly unique, as it involves both city and county governments and includes Columbia's neighboring communities on both sides of its rivers. In addition to the local government, organizations such as the Columbia Development Corporation, the Greater Columbia Chamber of Commerce, and the South Carolina Chamber of Commerce all are working together to encourage private investment in Columbia's development. These groups also share another goal—to recruit and retain profitable businesses in the Midlands region.

Architectural projects are keeping the city abuzz with activity as developers steadily build for the future. What once were old, dilapidated, yet historically significant buildings are now being transformed into beautiful and highly sought-after offices and living space. One such project gave new life to the Lutheran Survey Building. Located near North Main Street and close to the center of downtown, it was renovated to house a police substation and a community center to serve the neighborhood.

Another main focus for the downtown area is to develop modern projects while keeping an ambiance and historical appeal. This is what investors of the Lykes Building on Main Street in Columbia want to do. The building, constructed in 1906, originally included two stores on the ground floor with offices and residences on the upper floors. Architects marvel at the structure's rich history and charm, and with that in mind, private investors put a total of $500,000 into the project and worked to maintain the building's historic and structural authenticity.

Another nearby building has stood the test of time and has a makeover in its future. The old Armory at 1219 Assembly Street, also built in 1906, has been slated for an extensive restoration.

Existing businesses in the downtown area also are getting a fresh look. A new seven-story building now houses Carolina First—a much-needed expansion that is due to the bank's rapid growth. Carolina First shares a plaza with the newly relocated Columbia Museum of Art and has several other locations around the city for different bank departments.

The Columbia Museum of Art recently moved to the corner of Main and Hampton from its old location on the corner of Senate and Bull streets. At 80,000 square feet, it is the state's largest art museum and includes a 162-seat auditorium for concerts and lecture series. The museum houses rare and famous artwork and will provide an important economic boost for Main Street, the downtown community, and the entire Midlands area.

Another area of significant renovation is the Congaree Vista, located directly in downtown Columbia. Once a largely ignored area, investors found it ripe for development and renewal due to the large number of unique and historic buildings and warehouses. Thanks to this vision, today the area is a thriving community of businesses and residences.

The Vista also serves as a significant corridor connecting downtown with West Columbia, Cayce, and Lexington County. As part of the Vista's renovation, major streets such as Gervais now are bordered with blossoming pear trees, shrubbery, old-time street lamps, and flowers. These streets now play an important role as a scenic path to the city. To read more about the Vista's heritage and transformation, please turn to page 134.

〜 **Columbia residents can look forward to an array of cultural events at Koger Center, located on the campus of the University of South Carolina.** *Photo by Suzanne McGrane*

↩ **Revitalization has preserved the charm of Columbia's older neighborhoods and enhanced property values.** *Photo by Suzanne McGrane*

Up the street from the Vista sits the South Carolina State Capitol building, the site of another recent major renovation. The multimillion-dollar project was finished in 1998, and it involved restoring everything from the copper dome on top of the Capitol to the grand stairway leading into the building. As work progressed, hidden treasures surfaced, including a panel signed by the structure's original builders. Workers were also surprised to discover a live cannonball from the Civil War embedded in the building's thick stone walls—a relic of Gen. William T. Sherman's infamous attack.

Moving up Gervais Street and covering many city blocks, the University of South Carolina is gearing up for future growth. The school has several major projects under its belt and several more to come. For example, USC has expanded Williams-Brice Stadium—home of the Fighting Gamecocks football team. Huge crowds of fans were packing the stadium, so the school decided to upgrade its south end zone. The project features 7,600 additional seats, bringing stadium capacity to 80,250. Included in the addition is "The Zone"—an area of 1,600 premium club seats and a multi-purpose banquet room. This room has more than 11,000 square feet, giving the stadium more than 35,000 square feet of meeting space.

USC and local government entities also plan to enhance the city with a 20,000-seat arena, conference center, and private hotel in the Congaree Vista. The arena will be between 300,000 and 333,000 square feet and will seat between 18,500 and 20,000. It will be home to the Gamecock men's and women's basketball teams, as well as a professional hockey team. The

arena is scheduled to open in November 2002. All of these facilities will benefit the entire metro area by attracting conventioneers and sports enthusiasts to downtown.

Other higher education facilities also are participating in Columbia's development. With increased enrollment at two of Columbia's historically black colleges, the demand for student housing and administrative facilities has grown. In 1998, Benedict College purchased and renovated nearby town homes to provide living quarters for 175 students. And a new co-educational dorm that houses 230 students opened in August 1999.

Allen University, which is directly across the street from Benedict, also is making many improvements, including a facelift for the oldest building on campus. Arnette Hall, built in 1880, has undergone a federally funded renovation. The building houses several departments, along with a computer lab, archives, a chapel, and a soundproof recording room. Allen also is building a gymnasium and will begin renovations on the third-oldest building on campus, the Chappelle Administration Building. The rich cultural and academic history of both schools is certain to be enhanced by these projects. In addition, construction of the Barbara Bush Center for Science and Technology was recently completed at Columbia College, a historically all-women's liberal arts college to the north of downtown. The former first lady herself attended the opening of this state-of-the-art facility.

Columbia's renovations also involve older residential areas. Many of the area's historic communities have organized neighborhood associations so residents can work together to preserve and maintain their neighborhoods and individual houses. For instance, the Elmwood Park neighborhood has made a major commitment to maintaining historically significant assets of the community. Most of the Victorian-style homes have been renovated, and housing values have increased tremendously in this area.

One much-anticipated, large-scale project is taking shape on the former site of the Columbia Correctional Institution. Next to the Vista and within walking distance of its unique restaurants and shops, this once gray and foreboding place is now the site of a massive renovation and development project supported jointly by local governments. Beginning in 1997, the huge gray stones and red bricks of this facility were torn down to make way for a unique housing community, including condominiums, apartments, town houses and the River Inn hotel. Engineering has begun on-site and a six-year development plan has been divided into phases.

This one-of-a-kind urban living experience will be enhanced by completion of The Three Rivers Greenway, a project initiated by the River Alliance. The Alliance, a public-private effort to revitalize the Broad, Saluda, and Congaree rivers and surrounding areas, broke ground in the winter of 1998 for a 12-mile linear park that links the city to activities near the river.

A celebration area called the City Balcony, in connection with Three Rivers Greenway, will be in front of the hotel and river. This area will be an upscale esplanade with a pedestrian walkway, and it will link the children's museum and Riverfront Park. This prime location holds spectacular views of Columbia and of the confluence of the Saluda and Broad rivers. By the first years of the 21st century, it will be dotted with homes for families of varying incomes. All of these neighbors will have easy access to everything downtown has to offer and will share the opportunity to enjoy three of the nation's most unspoiled rivers.

Just across the Congaree by way of the Gervais Street Bridge, the city of West Columbia is also contributing to this area's transition into the future. Several new restaurants provide patrons with great views of the river, and antique shops are a common sight on historic State Street. Here, bargain hunters who enjoy the old and unusual can find hidden treasures inside older two-story buildings.

Other parts of the Columbia area have successfully maintained steady growth and development. Forest Drive, on the southeast side of Columbia,

**⌒ (Right) The Supreme Court of South Carolina building is one of Columbia's many architectural treasures.** *Photo by Suzanne McGrane*

**⌒ A number of large corporations have chosen to locate in the downtown area.** *Photo by Suzanne McGrane*

↶ The downtown area is home to many family-oriented activities, including the annual Carolina Carillon Christmas Parade. *Photo by Suzanne McGrane*

↶ (Left) Fresh produce and plants arrive daily at the State Farmers Market. *Photo by Suzanne McGrane*

is an example of the recent business explosion and the success of private investment in the community. Retail outlets are thriving in this section of town, due in large part to the Fort Jackson Army Base and the expansion of Interstate 77—the highway that leads travelers into the city of Columbia, up to Charlotte, North Carolina, and beyond to the Midwest.

The Harbison area also is experiencing rapid growth. Early investors recognized the potential of this area northwest of the city. These visionary developers knew they needed to plan with the future in mind. Their idea was to develop a diverse and economically integrated community, which they succeeded in doing. Today, Harbison offers Columbia residents modern and traditional-style homes in new and expanding subdivisions. Residents enjoy retail outlets like Columbiana Centre and the 140-acre Columbiana Station, which contains 400,000 square feet of retail space.

Expansion and revitalization are key strategies for the success of retail outlets and malls. Columbiana Centre is the youngest mall in the city and has attracted a high flow of customers. The mall has made some improvements and continues to add anchor and specialty stores. Columbia Mall and Richland Fashion Mall have also executed renovations. Dutch Square Center, one of the city's oldest malls, has been modernized and has experienced a huge increase in traffic flow. One new attraction at Dutch Square is a state-of-the-art movie theater that has 14 large screens, excellent digital sound, stadium-style seating, and loveseats. Other enhancements to Dutch Square include additional food tenants and retail outlets.

With all the renovation and development throughout the Columbia area, it's no wonder that this region is expected to keep growing by leaps and bounds. Projections for the year 2010 call for approximately 60,000 new residents, increasing the area population to more than 557,000. Columbia and the entire Midlands community are ready for this growth and eager to take on the challenges of the 21st century. And, Columbia can take pride in its accomplishments because the vision of its leaders and citizens has truly become a reality. ◙

↶ Golfers will find a range of challenging courses in the Columbia area. *Photo by Suzanne McGrane*

# The Vista: From Warehouses to Pubhouses

Home to quaint restaurants and shops, Columbia's Congaree Vista offers visitors and residents alike a diverse environment in an attractive warehouse district. Whether it's a night out on the town at one of the area's celebrated restaurants or an evening spent browsing for items not often associated with downtown shopping, the Vista offers a vast array of eclectic establishments.

Rich with historical significance, the Vista totals some 800 acres and covers the length of the Congaree River from Elmwood Avenue south to Blossom Street, and from Main Street east to the river. During the 1700s, the rivers that run through the city of Columbia were an essential means of transportation, trade, and business. Warehouses and mills were progressively built in areas along the river, while railroads transported items from city to city. By the early 20th century, the large tract of land below Assembly Street, also a part of the Columbia Historical District, had become a thriving economic center.

However, by the middle of the 20th century, Columbia's historical business district's economy had declined. With the emergence of new technology and more sophisticated modes of transportation, downtown and areas near the river had little business and few visitors or residents.

Fortunately, by the 1970s a resurgence of Main Street began to stimulate new public awareness about the central area. City planners started to see significance in the historical districts of Columbia and began to find ways to preserve Main Street and areas near the Congaree River. During the following years, what is now known as the Vista grew slowly into a revitalized community and a region of distinguished buildings. Today the Vista is a mixture of unique hidden residential areas, a thriving arts and antiques district, a $25-million State Museum, several community parks, and a host of other amenities.

Since 1905, planners have been developing strategies to improve Columbia, and they always emphasized the importance of the city's river-front development. One plan in particular encouraged businesses and landowners to remain in their present locations, and areas along West Gervais Street serve as prime examples of that plan's success. According to the South Carolina Department of Archives and History, this section of the Vista contains the largest number of long-established businesses in the city.

A transformation of the Mount Vernon Building is another example of what early city planners had hoped for. The former mill, located at the west end of Gervais Street on the banks of the Columbia Canal, now houses the South Carolina State Museum. The museum occupies more than half of the

⌒⌒ **Gervais Street has undergone a renaissance in recent years and is now home to many thriving businesses.** *Photo by Suzanne McGrane*

ᐤ **Older structures in the Vista area have been remodeled and now serve as pubs, restaurants, galleries, and shops.** *Photo by Suzanne McGrane*

old mill's floor space, and the wide-open floor plan that is several stories high allows visitors to appreciate the building's unique architecture. The dark wood beams and natural design features enhance the variety of exhibits covering cultural and natural history, science, technology, and art.

The African-American presence in the Vista also played an important role in development of the commercial district. During the early 1920s, the Washington Street business district developed from a residential area to a business center with 62 black-owned businesses, including restaurants, shops, and doctors' offices. Although many of the African-American businesses in the district are gone, plans are under way to preserve many of the buildings that housed some of these establishments. This revitalization effort has generated even more interest in preserving the Vista's heritage.

It seems as though once Columbia's citizens and out-of-town visitors experienced the Vista's rich history, they wanted to find a way to stay. Residents now live in lofts over shops, where they enjoy magnificent views of city lights and the river. Business owners have also decided to set up shop and stay for years to come. Although the Vista enjoys a solid future, the architectural past is preserved; only a few modern buildings have been built in the area.

The Vista's restaurants have century-old facades that convey an ambiance of the early 20th century, and each is unique in its decor and offerings. Many restaurants are situated in beautiful alleys with brick-paved streets that are lively with summertime activity. Music is almost always in the air since area restaurants often host an evening's entertainment on patios or in front of their establishments.

To contribute to the historic look of a commercial district, the City of Columbia revived the trolley system. The trollies, similar to buses but with all the characteristics of old-fashioned trolley cars, run every seven minutes on the midday route and every 20 minutes on the evening route. Riders get an opportunity to visit their favorite dining establishments during lunch hour, or they can be dropped off at one of the nightspots in the downtown area. Trolleys are also available for excursions within the greater Columbia area.

A highlight of each year is Vista Lights, a one-night event traditionally held in November that showcases local art and talent. During this night, Vista businesses host open houses for the community. Many art galleries in the district show off their studio space and works by local artists. Similarly, other creative shops and furniture merchants give guests a preview of their latest designs. Visitors can enjoy a number of activities during Vista Lights as they stroll along the streets or travel by trolley.

Beyond shopping and experiencing the great food and night life in the Vista, there is still more to do. Guided tours of the Congaree and Saluda rivers are popular adventures among residents and visitors alike. The area also features three major parks—one with a walking trail along the banks of the river, another with a waterfall overlooking downtown, and the third with picnic areas where bridges cross small streams.

Recently designed enhancements have turned the Vista into a spectator's dream. The city completed a facelift of Gervais Street, the major roadway in front of the famous Adluh Flour Company and the historic Ben Arnold Company. Beautiful trees now line the street and antique-style lighting fixtures adorn the area.

The Vista still contains large amounts of underutilized property, but city planners and groups are seeking ways to keep the area's historical value while fostering revitalization. Future development includes a world-class, hands-on, interdisciplinary children's museum, which is set to open in Spring 2001. The redevelopment of the Congaree River area will continue in the next few years as sites are designated for future homes, nature trails, and restaurants. Plans to transform an abandoned paper mill at one of the Vista's most popular intersections also are in the works. Developers hope to renovate the structure to house restaurants and shops.

The Congaree Vista possesses a colorful history, and its prospects are growing even brighter. As the Vista improves with age, it is sure to remain a place to explore the past, the present, and the future. ◪

ᐤ **Shoppers in the Congaree Vista will find a variety of treasures at shops such as City Market Antiques.** *Photo by Suzanne McGrane*

✍ The historic Adluh Flour Company has made its home in the Vista since 1900. *Photo by Suzanne McGrane*

✍ (Next page) A trolley heads up Gervais Street as night falls on the Vista. *Photo by Suzanne McGrane*

Part Two

Photo by Suzanne McGrane

# Chapter 9

## Education, Health Care & Quality of Life

Photo by Suzanne McGrane

# USC COLLEGE OF ENGINEERING & INFORMATION TECHNOLOGY

*A new name . . . a new vision . . . built on a foundation of excellence.*

As the flagship research university in the state, the University of South Carolina College of Engineering & Information Technology is an integral part of the Columbia community and state, providing expertise, resources, and lifelong learning opportunities for its citizens. From a modest beginning in 1894, the College has emerged a century later into a vibrant, innovative College that serves the engineering and technology needs of South Carolina through programs of education, research, and outreach. The College's high-quality educational and research programs attract the best students, vigorous businesses, and high-tech industries.

The College is committed to fostering the economic future through engineering education, research, innovation, and lifelong learning opportunities, and is dedicated to working collaboratively with business, industry, and government in finding new ways to meet South Carolina's needs in an increasingly technological environment.

In response to the state's critical need for experienced workers in the information technologies, the College established courses dedicated to Information Technology and changed its name to the College of Engineering & Information Technology. The new courses will enhance the fast-growing information technology industry by providing an educational program that will better prepare South Carolina's future workforce. With the merger of the University's Department of Computer Science into the College, the curriculum not only meets this demand, but will conduct leading-edge research in software engineering and network technology, and provide resources for other disciplines on campus. The College's faculty and graduate students are increasingly involved in research for existing industry and the College's new Technology Incubator supports the growth of new high-tech small businesses.

The College's initiatives in economic development—research partnerships with industry and collaboration with government to expand and support South Carolina's knowledge industries—will help create new jobs and a better quality of life for its citizens.

### Today's College not only predicts the future, but engineers it.

The College of Engineering & Information Technology is a national model for innovation and undergraduate education. Books, classrooms, and laboratory instruction are important, but so is the opportunity to apply what is learned. The College's undergraduate students have the unique opportunity to work with world-class researchers and graduate students on teams that will shape the landscape of the future. When the College began a century ago, founding fathers could not have anticipated the high-tech photonics and microelectronics laboratory, power electronics, fracture mechanics, fuel cells, and environmental engineering advancements that are an integral part of undergraduate study today. These opportunities for undergraduates and other research projects in the College indicate dedication to building world-class programs for the future on foundations laid by educators, researchers, and students of years past.

Through its seven programs, the College encourages future engineers to explore the excitement of engineering and technology. Through advanced

∽ **The Swearingen Engineering Center is a modern facility equipped with cutting-edge technology that supports education and research. Student computing facilities include five network servers and 112 PC workstations in four student computing labs. A high-performance network supports more than 800 high-end workstations for faculty and staff, leading software applications, local and remote access, a data network, and a world-class videoconference center.**

laboratories and facilities, and the latest in information technology, students and professional engineers can take courses for degrees or recertification anywhere, anytime, and on demand. Traditional and extended learning initiatives, scholarships, and a dedicated faculty attract top notch students from across the nation and the world, allowing the College to engineer the future.

Chemical Engineering turns raw materials in the form of chemicals into useful products, utilizing complex processing systems. Students work in research teams in the areas of fuel cells and advanced batteries that will revolutionize the transportation industry. They also can choose to work in the areas of composites technology, dense phase fluids, pharmaceuticals, polymers, plastics, advanced material development, nuclear energy, paper production, food processing, and design processes for a variety of areas, including the medical, cosmetic and textile industries.

With their research teams, Civil and Environmental Engineering students plan, design, and operate defense and civic-related structures and facilities, such as buildings and roads, transportation facilities, waterways, canals, dams, power plants, irrigation, water supply, airports, harbors, water and waste-water treatment plants, and power generation systems. Students work with professors to develop sensors that test the strength of aging infrastructure and create ways to sustain structures until repairs are complete. Developing ways to clean the air and the ground is a part of civil and environmental engineering students' curriculum, as is building and designing concrete canoes and bridges, and planning towns.

Electrical and Computer Engineering students work synergistically to provide power and software support for a variety of projects. Electrical engineers are concerned with energy creation, control, and handling; computer engineering deals with information creation and handling. Through the Photonics and Microelectronics Laboratory, students learn to produce wideband gap materials such as gallium nitride and silicon carbide that will enable computer chips to work with more power, better range, and greater tolerance for temperature extremes. Among other projects, Electrical Engineering students work with professors to design the power systems and Computer Engineering students design the computer animation programs that prototype complex naval power systems for evaluation.

Mechanical Engineering is the broadest focused of the engineering disciplines in that it incorporates many of the other engineering areas. Mechanical engineers design, build, and test all types of machinery and manufacture artifacts from toothpaste tubes to automobiles. Mechanical Engineers are involved with machines, manufacturing processes, mechanisms, engines, energy utilization, and energy conversion. They use computers in designing, testing, and evaluation. Among other areas, students can choose to work on teams that research advanced manufacturing operations and sustainable engineering, friction stir welding, kinetics, thermodynamics, robotics, computer-aided design (CAD), fracture mechanics, aerospace engineering, and vehicle design and performance.

∽ **These electrical engineering majors demonstrate their robotic-car project to Dr. Jerry Hudgins. This senior design lab is a course that incorporates mechanical, electrical, and software design engineering. As they will when they enter the workforce, students work in teams to develop written and oratory skills as part of their course requirements.**

frameworks. The program answers the question "Why do we have to learn this?" by showing children what they can do with their newfound knowledge of science and mathematics. Children in kindergarten and early grades will start to learn science, engineering, and math principles by playing with Lego bricks and similar toys. Older students will learn more about physics and math principles through interactive demonstrations of pulleys, levers, and similar devices. A progressively challenging series of engineering activities, from building Popsicle stick bridges in middle school to engineering design projects in high school, maintain students' interest and advance their knowledge of technology. The activities are fun, but this child's play is serious stuff. It's an introductory course that helps South Carolina's children learn about the practical application of the science and mathematics they learn in school. Whether they pursue careers in engineering or not, they will experience the excitement of invention, innovation, and complex problem solving—all great starting points to embark on the adventures of lifelong learning.

### The engineer in all of us.

One of the more serious challenges facing educators and, ultimately, industries that depend on engineers is making math, science, and engineering principles relevant to children in the early, formative years when they begin thinking about what they want to be when they grow up. Creating, inventing, improving, and modifying—that's what engineers do. Yet it's not uncommon for students and teachers to have little knowledge of what a career in engineering involves, in terms of disciplines and the types of problem engineers work on.

Throughout the decade, the College has worked closely with high-school and middle-school teachers and classes to let students experience the excitement of engineering. Now the College has added new programs for younger children. The result is a comprehensive program, The Engineer in All of Us, that makes interactive engineering projects available to science teachers in all grade levels and provides an array of resources for students and schools. "Our society is becoming more focused on technology, yet fewer children are interested in engineering as a career," says Dr. Joseph Gibbons, associate dean for academics. "In order for society and our state's economy to be strong and secure, we must inspire children to be a part of the technology workforce."

Every day during the school year, the College's Engineer in All of Us van is at a school where the program's coordinator works with teachers in demonstrating interactive engineering principles based on the state's science

### Professional education for engineers—anytime, anywhere, on demand.

Continuing professional development graduate classes, strategically located around South Carolina, provide graduate engineering education for professional engineers through videoconferencing that allows them to confer with their professors during videoconference hours. These technology-enabled classes allow engineers to meet professional certification requirements, keep up with advances in technology and theory, upgrade management skills, and earn an advanced degree at a location convenient to them.

The College's multi-media and telecommunications system that merges video, audio, and data sharing, combined with the student's low-cost hardware and software provided by the College, gives them videoconference capability, making every professor's office a conference room and every student's PC a classroom. Classes provide instruction through digital material, CD-ROM, web-based material, and other multi-media communications methods.

### Engineering South Carolina's future.

The College's vision and mission to become a national model for innovation and responsiveness in addressing the engineering education, economic development, and lifelong learning needs of South Carolina are deeply rooted for the millennium. Through its innovative programs, dedicated world-class faculty, and achievement-oriented students, the College of Engineering & Information Technology is well positioned to Engineer South Carolina's future. ◪

# BENEDICT COLLEGE

⌒ **Dr. David H. Swinton, president and CEO of Benedict College.**

Founded in 1870 by Rhode Island native Bathsheba Benedict, Benedict College was an 80-acre plantation when purchased as the Benedict Institute. The investors—Mrs. Benedict and the Baptist Home Mission—had a long-term goal of educating emancipated African-Americans and producing citizens who were "powers for good in society."

Over 130 years later, Benedict College is the fastest growing of 39 United Negro College Fund Schools and is ranked first in the state of the private undergraduate institutions. More than 2,700 students currently study at the school, and that figure is expected to reach 3,000 (its largest enrollment) by 2005.

The school's growth is more than an expanding student enrollment. Benedict College is also involved in an ambitious building program. The campus at the corner of Harden and Taylor Streets has recently undergone substantial renovations to its Antisdel Chapel, the Benjamin E. Mays Human Resource Center, Morgan Hall, Pratt Hall, and most of the dormitories.

But the school's growth is not limited to its historic area. Benedict College is also erecting a multimillion-dollar, 60-acre sports complex off Two Notch Road in Columbia. The new facility will include tennis courts, baseball fields, fitness trails, a running track, and a large football stadium. The school's

long-term goal is to add property and build facilities to connect the main campus and the athletic center.

Football returned to Benedict College three years ago after a 30-year hiatus. And with football came its complement, the marching band. While credited by some as a boost to male student enrollment, according to Dr. David H. Swinton, president of Benedict College, the move back to football was a way for students to feel a "community *esprit de corps*," and boost the "spirit and quality of the school."

The school has attracted other successes which speak to spirit and quality. The average SAT scores, Honors College enrollee rate, capital giving dollars, and the number of research grants awarded to Benedict College have all increased. Also growing are the numbers of valedictorians and high achievers making the school their first choice for higher education.

Students attending Benedict College have the opportunity to earn a four-year, liberal arts degree from 23 different disciplines. These include accounting, art, biology, business administration, chemistry, child and family development, computer science, computer/information science, criminal justice, early childhood education, economics, elementary education, English, environmental health science, history, mathematics, music education, physics, political science, recreation, religion and philosophy, and social work.

But receiving an academic education is only a part of the Benedict College experience. Service to the community also defines its students. Each undergraduate is required to complete 120 hours of service training as part of his or her educational experience.

To help its students encourage their communities toward fairness and equality, Benedict College started The Center of Excellence for Community Development in 1997. This center is comprised of four programs:

⌒ **Benedict College gives its students access to the latest technology. Its student-to-computer ratio is 10 to 1, which is above the national average.**

～ **The majority of Benedict College's students live on campus, and dormitories are equipped with cable and internet access.**

educational excellence, the child and family (excellence) program, business and economic development, and democracy and government. Each program is designed to help solve a distinct set of problems afflicting American society and in particular, African-Americans.

The goal of the education excellence program is to improve the standardized test scores and overall performances of African-American students. Innovative test-taking skills will be taught to participating students, using a variety of life experiences as teaching and learning aids. African-American student performance improvement will assist the program in reaching another important goal—high-school student drop-out rate reduction.

Solving problems associated with growing up in a disadvantaged home is the mission of the child and family (excellence) program. This part of the excellence center develops strategies, tactics, and programs to help African-Americans deal with problems related to poverty, drug addiction, and child abuse.

Encouraging small business ownership and business improvement, particularly among African-Americans, is the goal of the business and economic development program. This excellence center focuses on teaching the principles and practices of entrepreneurship and equates ownership with empowerment.

Community participation in the governmental process is the overall goal of the democracy and government portion of the Benedict College Center of Excellence. Of particular interest are the efforts this program makes to encourage voting. The eventual goal is to "enable our American democracy to work effectively not just for some of its people, but for all of its people," said Swinton.

Benedict College has a long history of producing high achievers. Some notable alumni include Major General Matthew Zimmerman and Dr. LeRoy Walker, president emeritus of the U.S. Olympic Committee. Other distinguished graduates include I.S. Leevy Johnson Esquire, the first African-American president of the South Carolina Bar Association; Modjeska Simkins, often referred to as the mother of the South Carolina civil rights movement; and Maria Pyles, the 1990 South Carolina Teacher of the Year and National Teacher of the Year finalist.

Benedict College has also hosted many distinguished entertainers and visitors as part of its performing arts and lecture programs, including Tremain Hawkins,

Eartha Kitt, Clifton Davis, and Julianna Malveau. Events for student, faculty, and the community hosted by Benedict College include Soulful Noel holiday concerts, African-American bazaars, and town hall meetings on community and race relations.

Columbia's businesses and institutions have noticed the school's progress. Benedict College enjoys healthy relationships with many of them, including Policy Management Systems Corporation, The Medical University of South Carolina, Freddie Mac (the Federal Home Mortgage Corporation), Wachovia Bank, Bank of America, Carolina First, Colonial Life, Chatham Steel Corporation, SCANA Corporation, and others.

"From our post-Civil War beginnings, our institution has had an eye to the future, serving as a beacon of hope for those who had little but wanted to contribute much. We are a school dedicated to affording students the opportunity for full participation in a highly competitive American society," said Swinton. ❧

～ **Benedict College is proud of its 15-to-1 student/faculty ratio. Its students receive close attention from the college's distinguished faculty, 75 percent of whom have earned PhDs.**

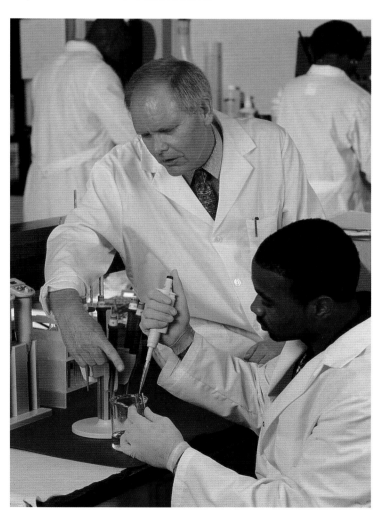

# PALMETTO HEALTH ALLIANCE

🖎 (Above) Palmetto Health Alliance hospitals include Palmetto Baptist Medical Center in Columbia and Easley, and Palmetto Richland Memorial Hospital in Columbia. Each year, the hospitals treat nearly a half million patients. With a combined employee population in excess of 7,500 people, Palmetto Health is the largest health care system in the state and the seventh largest employer in the state. *Photos by Brian Dressler and George Fulton*

Health care in South Carolina leaped forward with the creation of Palmetto Health Alliance in February 1998. By combining the resources of three respected South Carolina hospitals—Palmetto Baptist Medical Center and Palmetto Richland Memorial Hospital in Columbia and Palmetto Baptist Medical Center in Easley—Palmetto Health helped ensure continued advancements in services and facilities for Columbia and beyond.

Each year, the hospitals of Palmetto Health treat nearly half a million patients, welcome more than 6,000 babies into the world, and make nearly 120,000 home care visits. With more than 1,200 beds and more than 7,500 employees, including a 1,000-member medical and dental staff, Palmetto Health is South Carolina's largest health care system and one of the state's largest employers. It is a nonprofit organization governed by a locally appointed board of directors.

Palmetto Health's areas of clinical excellence include cancer, behavioral medicine, cardiology, geriatrics, neurosciences, obstetrics (including high-risk pregnancy and genetic counseling), orthopedics, pediatrics, surgery, trauma, and women's services. In many of these areas, Palmetto Health serves as the

🖎 Palmetto Health's CareForce helicopter is the only flying critical care unit of its kind and size in the Midlands. The helicopter, which is used to transport critically ill and injured patients from remote areas to health care facilities in Columbia, is uniquely equipped to transport infants and is large enough for two adult patients. *Photo by Rick Smoak*

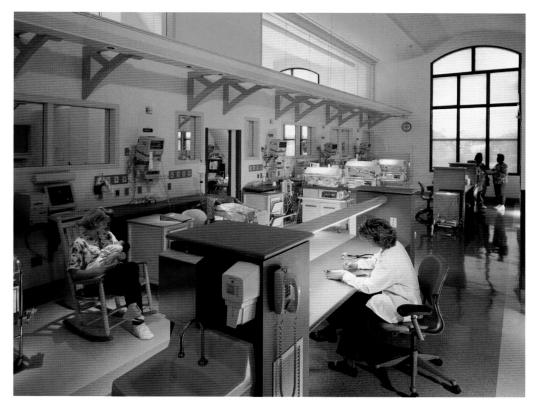

Palmetto Health also devotes enormous resources to community programs designed to keep people well and out of the hospital. Health fairs, screenings, support groups, workshops, and seminars sponsored by the hospitals' service lines are invaluable sources of information and support for the community. A prime example is Palmetto Baptist's PrimeTimes program for older adults. This popular program attracted more than 17,000 members in its first decade of operation.

In addition, a full 10 percent, or $3.5 million, of Palmetto Health's bottom line is designated each year as a "community tithe" to fund development and implementation of programs with potential to directly improve community health. These initiatives continue the legacy of progress established by Palmetto Health's anchor hospitals, Palmetto Baptist and Palmetto Richland, during more than two centuries of combined service. The result is clinical health care excellence enhanced by a tradition of caring and research.

∽ The Level III Neonatal Intensive Care Unit at Palmetto Richland Memorial Hospital offers the highest level of newborn critical care available in the Midlands and is a regional referral center for this specialized area of care. The NICU is one of only two in South Carolina with Extra Corporeal Membrane Oxygenation, a life-saving heart-lung bypass machine for newborns. Palmetto Baptist Medical Center also operates a Level III NICU in the Midlands, providing expert care to premature or sick infants. *Photo by George Fulton*

regional referral center for the Midlands, often drawing patients from around the state, or for some specialties, from around the world.

Patients who receive care at Palmetto Health hospitals and facilities also benefit from the organization's strong affiliation with the University of South Carolina that includes research partnerships with the USC School of Medicine and 11 physician residency programs. Palmetto Health's commitment to maintaining a teaching hospital ensures its patients have access to a complete range of treatment methods and research. In fact, in 1999, Palmetto Health Alliance and the University of South Carolina formed a collaboration called the South Carolina Cancer Center (SCCC). The SCCC is one of the largest comprehensive cancer programs in the Southeast.

Other notable features of Palmetto Health include a network of physician practices throughout the Midlands, 24 pastoral counseling centers across the state, six day-health centers located throughout the Midlands to serve medically fragile older adults, and a day-health center in Columbia for medically fragile children. Palmetto Health also operates CareForce, the region's only air medical transport helicopter equipped to handle critically ill newborns as well as adult trauma patients.

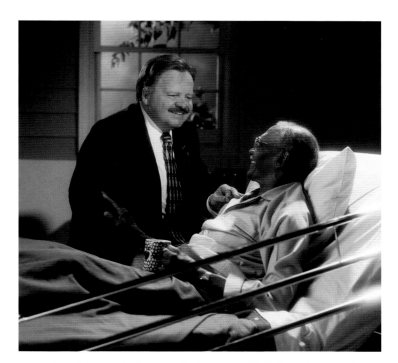

∽ Chaplains are just one part of the multidisciplinary team that supports patients in the Palmetto Health Hospice program serving 21 counties across South Carolina. Chaplains also visit inpatients in Palmetto Health hospitals. *Photo by George Fulton*

# PROVIDENCE HOSPITAL

*Morning and evening prayers over the public address system remind patients, visitors, physicians, volunteers, and staff of the Christian mission of the Sisters.*

Providence Hospital is located in downtown Columbia at 2435 Forest Drive and has been offering a wide variety of medical care services in a Catholic setting since 1938.

Compassion, respect, caring—these are all words that live within the heart of Providence Hospital's mission. The downtown hospital was built more than 60 years ago through the generosity of the Sisters of Charity of St. Augustine. The Sisters, who resided in Cleveland, Ohio, mortgaged their mother house because they believed so much in the need for Providence Hospital. And today, Providence has grown to accommodate the community's need for a broader spectrum of health care services.

"Our mission," says Stephen A. Purves, president and CEO, "is to meet the health care needs of the community by an expression of Christian concern for the sick, suffering, and dying; to manifest love, truth, and justice in health care; and to promote the advancement and application of new knowledge about health care. That remains the spirit that guides us today."

Dedication to medical advancement and innovation is reflected at Providence Heart Institute, located at the downtown campus, where heart specialists perform diagnostic work, interventional heart procedures, and open-heart surgery. Providence Hospital is ranked among the top 10 percent of open-heart surgery programs in the United States.

✎ **Life Reach, South Carolina's first hospital-based helicopter ambulance, is Providence Hospital's airborne intensive care unit, which ensures that people anywhere in South Carolina have access to advanced critical/cardiac care.** *Photo by P. Crawford*

Providence Hospital/Heart Institute is recognized as a "Center of Excellence" for its role as a leading referral center for prevention, diagnosis, and treatment of cardiovascular disease.

Another groundbreaking program at Providence is Life Reach, the hospital's airborne intensive care unit, which ensures that people anywhere in South Carolina have access to advanced critical/cardiac care. Life Reach, South Carolina's first hospital-based helicopter ambulance, was established in March 1985. Staffed with a highly skilled nurse, paramedic, and pilot, Life Reach transports an average of 55 cardiac and trauma patients each month. The helicopter is staffed and ready to respond to calls from physicians, EMS, and law enforcement 24 hours a day.

*Other signature hospital services include:*

*General/Orthopedic Surgery:* Physicians at Providence perform more than 5,000 surgical procedures a year, including orthopedic, plastic, otolaryngology (ear, nose, and throat), and much more.

*Outpatient Surgery:* Providence combines state-of-the-art surgical attention with the convenience and cost-efficiency of same-day service.

*Ophthalmology Care:* A recognized leader in eye care, Providence offers the latest diagnostic and surgical services at Providence Eye Surgery Center.

*The Sleep Sciences Center:* The center diagnoses and treats a wide variety of sleep disorders as diverse as REM behavior disorders, nocturnal seizures, and narcolepsy.

Enhancing the specialty care available at the main campus is the focus on family medicine offered at Providence Hospital's northeast facility.

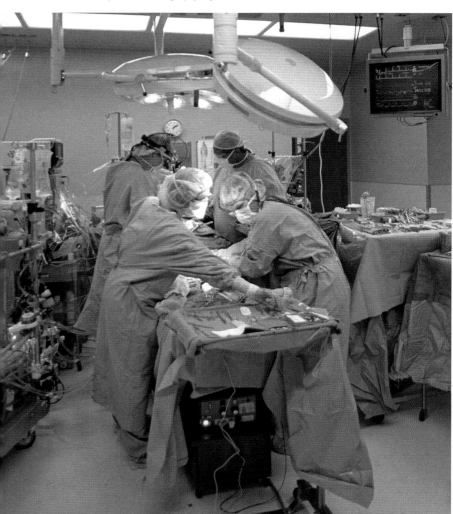

✎ **Dedication to medical advancement and innovation is reflected at Providence Heart Institute, located at the downtown campus, where heart specialists perform diagnostic work, interventional heart procedures, and open-heart surgery.** *Photo by P. Crawford*

〜 Compassion, respect, caring—these are all words that live within the heart of Providence Hospital's mission. *Photo by P. Crawford*

CPR, and more, while the Providence chapter of "Senior Friends," one of 225 throughout the United States, offers monthly meetings, social and travel opportunities, and health screenings to area residents ages 50 and older.

Growing families may take advantage of parenting classes, stress management workshops, and, just for children, "Providence Kids' Club," a monthly program for kids ages 7 through 12 designed to spotlight safety and health issues through fun activities.

For all ages and all health needs, Providence Hospital continues the commitment to the community and to the mission set forth by the Sisters when they opened the hospital in 1938. Providence Hospital—mending hearts and more. **G**

***The main doors of Providence Hospital Northeast open and a new mother is wheeled out to a waiting car, with flowers, balloons, and beaming family members in tow.***

This represents a common scene for many hospitals, but for Columbia, it also represents the return of Providence Hospital-born babies. Indeed, Providence Hospital Northeast, opened to the public in late March 1999, devotes its entire third floor to maternity services. Labor/delivery/recovery/postpartum rooms ensure that the expectant mother does not have to be moved at any point during the delivery process. The maternity floor even has its own separate entrance to allow women and their families a greater level of privacy and convenience. And every time a baby is born at Providence Hospital Northeast, the hospital plays "Brahms' Lullaby" throughout the facility to celebrate the arrival of a new little life.

Other services at Providence Northeast include emergency care, diagnostic services, inpatient/outpatient surgery, transitional care, and wound care services. The Transitional Care Unit admits patients who have been discharged from the hospital but still require rehabilitative or subacute care. The Wound Care Services program offers individualized attention and therapy for hard-to-heal wounds.

Providence Hospital Northeast is located in the Gateway Corporate Center development off I-77 North between Hard Scrabble Road and Highway 555, one of Columbia's most rapidly growing areas. Connected to this facility is Providence Medical Office Plaza, an 80,000-square-foot facility featuring orthopedic, family, OB-Gyn, and other medical specialties.

Innovation and individualized attention are integrated into every aspect of care at both Providence Hospital and Providence Hospital Northeast. And reaching out to the community is part of that concern.

As Americans are living longer, Providence has developed programs and areas of care that focus on the preventive aspects of health. Community health education programs cover issues such as high blood pressure, proper diet,

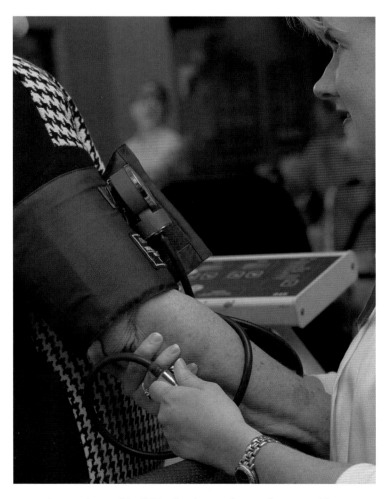

〜 Innovation and individualized attention are integrated into every aspect of care at both Providence Hospital and Providence Hospital Northeast. *Photo by P. Crawford*

# BLUE CROSS AND BLUE SHIELD OF SOUTH CAROLINA

Say "Blue Cross" and most people think health insurance. But Blue Cross and Blue Shield of South Carolina offers the people of Columbia, the state of South Carolina, and the nation so much more.

From origins in 1946 as a provider of hospital insurance only, Blue Cross today stands as the state's largest health care insurer—offering a variety of health plans for individuals, small businesses, and large groups. A leader in managed care, Blue Cross operates the state's largest network of healthcare providers—Preferred Blue. It also gives its customers a choice of two health maintenance organizations (HMOs), Companion HealthCare and HMO Blue.

Benefit design is only one of Blue Cross' core competencies. Technology is another. In 1998 Blue Cross completed a major enhancement to its data center. Fewer than 50 data centers worldwide process at its technology level.

Blue Cross shares that technical expertise with the federal government. Through its subsidiary, Palmetto Government Benefits Administrators, L.L.C., Blue Cross has become one of the largest administrators of government health insurance contracts—Medicare and TRICARE—in the nation.

Blue Cross also operates several subsidiaries that take advantage of the company's expertise in benefit design, technology, and more.

Two of those subsidiaries are insurance companies—Companion Life Insurance Company and Companion Property and Casualty Insurance Group.

Companion Life markets life, disability, and dental insurance programs. Companion Property and Casualty offers property and casualty insurance programs, and is a leader in the workers' compensation arena.

Companion Technologies and Companion Information Management Resources (CIMR) bring the benefits of electronic commerce to Blue Cross' customers, especially healthcare provider partners. Companion Technologies offers hardware and software that lets providers send claims and gather benefit information electronically, efficiently, and economically.

∿ **Blue Cross and Blue Shield has a significant economic impact on Columbia and the state of South Carolina. During the last decade, Blue Cross saw its employee base more than triple.**

CIMR offers advanced systems that let healthcare groups or other insurance companies track, manage, and see their patients' total healthcare picture—all at the push of a button.

Companion Benefit Alternatives, Companion Capital Management, and Planned Administrators Inc. (PAI) round out the Blue Cross family of subsidiaries. Companion Benefit Alternatives manages the mental health benefits for people in group health plans. Companion Capital Management directs the financial portfolios of major corporations. PAI handles claims administration for large companies who self fund their insurance plans.

All of these programs and subsidiaries translate into thousands of jobs—and a significant economic impact—on Columbia and the state of South Carolina. During the last decade of the twentieth century, Blue Cross saw its employee base more than triple. And Blue Cross is always hiring talented, dedicated team members—from computer programmers who keep the computer systems running to customer service representatives who keep customers happy.

As a good corporate citizen, Blue Cross contributes substantially to its communities. From high-dollar contributions to worthy causes to the hands-on commitment of employees building homes for Habitat for Humanity, Blue Cross makes its presence known to all of the public it serves. Blue Cross doesn't simply market insurance—it makes an impression! ◼

∿ **From origins in 1946 as a provider of hospital insurance only, Blue Cross and Blue Shield of South Carolina today stands as the state's largest healthcare insurer—offering a variety of health plans for individuals, small businesses, and large groups.**

# YMCA

Spirit, mind, and body form the framework for the Young Men's Christian Association nationwide. In 1854, the Columbia YMCA was formed as one of the first 50 YMCAs in the country. Fifty-seven years later, Governor Woodrow Wilson of New Jersey, a future president, laid the cornerstone of the current structure. Few imagined how the innovative energy of the organization would impact the Greater Columbia area in years to come.

Today, the Columbia YMCA holds strong to its Christian foundation as it flourishes into the new millennium. In doing so, it also provides a comprehensive range of health enhancement, sports, and community service for men and women, boys and girls, from all walks of life.

The Columbia YMCA has long been known for its pioneering efforts in youth and adult fitness and wellness programs. In 1972, it also pioneered the tremendous growth of soccer in South Carolina by introducing the Midland's first organized youth soccer league. The Y's soccer league remains one of the largest and most respected programs in the area. The Y also offers baseball, basketball, golf, lacrosse, tennis, and volleyball, and the Y's Sports Department has received the Governor's Council on Physical Fitness Award for consistent excellence in promoting fitness, character development, and good sportsmanship. Participants in the Y's 70-plus-year-old Sunday School Basketball program must attend at least 50 percent of Sunday school classes at their church or synagogue, an example of the Y's emphasis on priorities.

The aquatics program offers a variety of services as well. In addition to helping youth and adult students of all ages learn to swim, the Y also provides lifeguard training and certification, CPR certification, water aerobics, and a fast growing youth swim team. With the completion of the Columbia

ᑖ **The YMCA Youth Incentive Program (YIP) rewards students for improved behavior, effort, and attitude in their schools.**

NorthWest Family YMCA, the 8-lane indoor pool offers year-round training for its swim team.

In keeping with its pledge to "build strong kids, strong families, strong communities," the Y-Indian Guide and Princess program exemplifies the Columbia YMCA's commitment to families. In this, fathers are given the opportunity to learn how to guide, teach, and communicate lessons of life to their children through organized neighborhood activities and fall and spring campouts. Family Nights and Parents' Night Out are some of the regular highlights at branch locations.

The after-school program gives parents a different kind of day care. The Y runs its programs inside several grade schools and at the 160-acre Family Center near the city of Lexington. Students engage in learning experiences such as nature hikes, canoeing, sports, and crafts. The Y's National Character Development program helps the children to realize, utilize, and develop their own unique gifts and talents. It also allows teens to gain and learn how to handle responsibility as they proceed into their adult lives.

Through its various programs, the Columbia YMCA is also recognized as a leader in providing community services—many of them aimed at disadvantaged youth. The Youth Incentive Program, for example, is a free service for inner city youth whose families may not be financially secure but want their children to experience a positive and moral environment. And in the Black Achievers Program, which started in Harlem, successful African-American adults volunteer as mentors and are role models to young people. Financial assistance and scholarships are available for families who need assistance in the Y's sports, camping, childcare, and other programs.

Today, through the outstanding lay leadership of community-spirited volunteers and the efforts of a dedicated professional staff, the Columbia YMCA continues to build well-rounded individuals. And it does so by adhering to the principles that have guided it from the beginning: Providing men and women of all ages, races, religions, and economic standing the opportunity to better themselves in spirit, mind, and body. ᑕ

ᑖ **The 160-acre YMCA Family Center offers an equestrian program, a 12-acre pond, weatherized cabins, a dining hall, and other accommodations for year-round enjoyment.**

# MIDLANDS TECHNICAL COLLEGE

Midlands Technical College's reputation in the Central Midlands of South Carolina as a significant source of education, job training, and continuing education is unexcelled. Founded in 1963, Midlands Technical College (MTC) is a multicampus, public, two-year college offering the associate degree, diploma, and certificate in a variety of career training and college transfer programs. Each fall, MTC serves approximately 10,000 students in college credit programs and more than 34,000 others through its continuing education division.

Midlands Technical College's academic departments offer more than 85 programs of study. About one of every three college-bound high-school graduates in the college's service area enrolls at MTC, and the college is the largest source of transfer students to the University of South Carolina.

MTC graduates are educated to be competitive in the job market, self-confident in their pursuits, and capable of making significant contributions to their community. The college's commitment to excellence is evident in its students' success. Nearly 100 percent of MTC graduates available for employment are employed or continuing their education six months after graduation. Ninety-seven percent of surveyed employers rate MTC graduates as good or excellent.

The high student success rate at MTC would not be possible without an equally impressive faculty and staff. Eighty-three percent of the faculty hold master's or doctorate degrees in their teaching fields. The college's small class sizes make it possible for students to receive individualized attention from MTC's dedicated instructors. Many of these faculty members have received teaching awards on the national, regional, and state levels.

∽ **Students socialize in a courtyard at Midlands Technical College.**

Midlands Technical College currently has three sites: Beltline Campus in Richland County, and Airport Campus and Harbison Campus in Lexington County. Property has been purchased adjacent to the Carolina Research Park in Richland County. This Northeast site will house the college's Technology Training Center, which will offer state-of-the-art responses to the Midlands region's demand for skilled computer and high-technology employees.

MTC's successes are due to its innovation, close cooperation with business and industry, and flexible responses to economic challenges. In keeping with its commitment to the economic development of the Central Midlands of South Carolina, MTC establishes early and sustained contact with all businesses and industries considering relocation or expansion to the Midlands. The college's academic and continuing education programs are developed in close consultation with business, industry, and the Central Midlands community. For more than 35 years, MTC has been a vital partner in the region's economic growth.

Midlands Technical College enters the 21st century with a continued commitment to providing high-quality educational opportunities to the citizens of South Carolina's Central Midlands and to promoting economic growth and well-being among the Midlands' businesses and industries. By building on its history of success, MTC will continue to be a part of Columbia's competitive advantage for the future. ◪

∽ **Midlands Technical College Airport Student Center**

Photo by Suzanne McGrane

# Chapter 10

## Marketplace

Photo by Suzanne McGrane

# EMBASSY SUITES

A marvelous lush green atrium and smiling faces welcome travelers as they glide through the magnificent revolving doors of Columbia's Embassy Suites. Immediately, Embassy Suites staff members are on hand to assist guests with room accommodations and anything else they can do to make their guests feel welcome at their home away from home. And whether it is an excited family of four on vacation or the tired business person in town for a meeting, Embassy Suites is committed to helping them feel secure, satisfied, and happy.

Columbia's Embassy Suites is located off I-126 at the Greystone Boulevard exit, three miles from downtown, 15 miles from the Columbia Metropolitan Airport, and just down the street from the expansive Riverbanks Zoo and Botanical Garden; and the staff at the luxury hotel guarantees their guests high-quality accommodations, friendly and efficient service, and clean, comfortable surroundings.

Embassy Suites is committed to an unconditional guarantee that ensures its guests' complete satisfaction, whenever they stay in Columbia, or at any of its other 142 locations inside or outside the United States. The people at Embassy Suites will do everything possible to ensure that their guests get a good night's sleep and wake up refreshed.

But it is very hard to find a reason not to be satisfied. After guests get their service with a smile when they are greeted at the door, they are ready to check into their spacious, deluxe two-room suites designed to improve productivity for business travelers while providing comfort and flexibility for vacationers. Each elegant room comes with a separate, spacious living room with a convenient fold-out sofa bed for extra family members or guests; comfortable seating for relaxing after a tiring day of meetings or at the zoo with the kids; lots of space for quick or in-depth business meetings, dine-in meals, fun games, and late-night conversation; private bedroom with a king-size bed or two double beds for a good night's sleep; coffeemaker, refrigerator, microwave, and wet-bar— great for quick snacks; two remote-controlled televisions, one in each room; two telephones, each with modem capabilities; iron and ironing board in each suite; choice of smoking or nonsmoking accommodations; and services for guests with disabilities, including roll-in showers and beds on frames.

In addition, each guest will enjoy a complimentary, cooked-to-order breakfast to start the morning off right and a complimentary newspaper delivered to their suite door each weekday morning. Embassy Suites offers 214 of these stylish, grand two-room suites that present an ideal escape from a busy day.

Guests who venture out of their rooms after unpacking and filling up on the wet-bar or some television will find numerous amenities throughout the hotel. These include a heated, sparkling indoor pool, a whirlpool for that relaxing dip at the end of the day, and a sauna. For the exercise enthusiast, Embassy Suites offers fully equipped exercise facilities with state-of-the-art weight machines, bicycles, treadmills, rowing machines, and much more. Each evening, guests are invited to relax and unwind at a special guest reception.

Hungry guests will find many dining opportunities at Embassy Suites Columbia, and hotel chefs take extra care to ensure food service excellence that each guest can see and savor. The 110-seat Park Place Restaurant serves delicious culinary delights on a bistro-style menu for lunch and dinner. And on the weekends, the bistro serves up a delectable Sunday brunch. Guests can enjoy their favorite slice from Pizza Hut at Park Place or through Embassy Suites' suite service. Pizzas are made fresh and hot in Embassy Suites' very own Pizza Hut kitchen.

The Fountain Court Lounge allows guests to enjoy elegant conversation while they sip on a cappuccino or other favorite beverage and enjoy some tasty appetizers. This warm, comfortable piano bar atmosphere is nestled in the corner of the delightful atrium with its lush foliage and waterfalls. It is designed to be a very relaxing part of a guest's stay at Embassy Suites.

Embassy Suites Columbia is part of the largest all-suite, upscale hotel chain in the country. The Embassy Suites Columbia is the first built and managed by John Q. Hammons Hotels Inc.; the hotel is just minutes from Columbia's featured attractions and lively downtown. The seven-story building also is a perfect

∽ **Greystone Hall**

meeting place for company conferences and meetings. With 16,000 square feet of flexible meeting space, Embassy Suites is eager to host meetings and conferences. The hotel, with its sun-drenched atrium that is perfect for relaxing in between meetings, offers seven fully equipped board rooms for smaller meetings or break-out rooms.

Meetings can also be planned on-line. An interactive service allows the flexibility and power to coordinate meeting details on-line. The "Plan a Meeting" icon on the Embassy Suites' web site allows guests to request

∽ **Guest Suite**

equipment will be set up on time and in excellent working order. Guests will be presented with accurate documentation of billing in a timely fashion.

For that lovely wedding reception or end-of-the-year, black-tie banquet, Embassy Suites presents the glorious Greystone Hall. The 3,100-square-foot hall is a designer's showcase of brilliance and elegance.

And it is Embassy Suites' revolving door of quality service, which translates to 100 percent customer satisfaction and a "design for living," that helps it stand above the rest. What's more, J.D. Power & Associates ranked Embassy Suites highest overall in guest satisfaction among all-suites hotel chains for 1999.

Embassy Suites employs people who have that satisfaction guarantee ingrained in their own philosophy and work ethic. The company values a service-minded attitude as highly as any other job skill. Prospective employees must have a vision to satisfy the guests. One thing that makes Embassy Suites different is its entire staff's commitment to that 100 percent satisfaction guarantee, making sure that each quest is 100 percent satisfied. Their boss IS the guest. It is no wonder guests keep coming back. ⊄

⤳ **Garden Atrium**

sleeping room blocks and schedule an entire week's agenda. Each request receives a response within 24 hours.

At Embassy Suites, the all-star staff gives every meeting its full attention, no matter how big or small. The staff delivers high-quality meeting areas; friendly, attentive service; quality, timely food and beverage delivery; fully operational audiovisual equipment per guest specifications; and accurate, timely billing.

To demonstrate its commitment to the success of its guests' meetings, Embassy Suites offers the following assurances: A designated hotel representative will be assigned to each meeting to assist throughout the entire function in any way. Meeting rooms will be available for use when promised and set up to guest specifications before the start of the meeting, and this includes proper control of sound, lighting, heating, air-conditioning, and ventilation. Refreshment breaks for meetings will be set up to meet guest specifications and delivered on time. Catered meal functions will be served according to guest specifications; hot food will be served hot, cold food served cold all at times requested. Audio and visual

⤳ **Pool and Spa**

# GALEANA CHRYSLER-PLMOUTH-JEEP-KIA

S"Service" and "consistency" are important words at Galeana Chrysler-Plymouth-Jeep-Kia. So important, in fact, that they form the basis of the dealership's mission statement, which hangs prominently in the dealer offices on Greystone Boulevard. It is that very commitment to service and consistency, to their customers and staff, and to the community that has made the dealership such a permanent fixture in Columbia since it was opened in June 1988.

In the late 1960s, Frank Galeana started with a small loan and a big dream of his own car dealership. Some 30 years later, the Galeana Automotive Group is the 75th largest dealership chain in the country, and its Columbia location is one of the company's brightest stars. The largest dealership of its kind in South Carolina, Galeana is proud of its selection of over 500 new and preowned cars and trucks, a 25,000-square-foot showroom, a 30,000-square-foot service and parts department, and a state-of-the-art, 12,500-square-foot body shop.

After years of success, Frank Galeana's philosophy hasn't changed. Service and consistency are still the two words that matter most.

### Commitment to Customer Service

Chrysler luxury cars and minivans. Value-conscious cars from Plymouth. Sport-utility vehicles (SUVs) from Jeep. Economy-minded imported cars, vans, and compact SUVs from Kia. Galeana's brand-name products stretch across the entire automotive spectrum, and buyers won't have any trouble finding a model that suits their tastes and needs. Just ask 20,000 of their clients in Columbia.

What is the secret of their success? It's simple. Customers matter to the people at Galeana. So much so that the dealership—unlike many other dealers—employs a full-time Customer Relations Manager who focuses solely on meeting customer post-sales needs.

∽ The Galeana facility on Greystone Boulevard.

In the last few years, Galeana has invested even more time and money into strengthening what was an already successful dealership. Five years ago, Galeana unveiled a world-class body shop, filled with the latest technology.

Problem repairs don't take weeks at Galeana. The service department is now home to some of the finest repair equipment available, including satellite capabilities that allow Galeana's service technicians to ask for and quickly receive repair tips from the engineering department at the Chrysler Corporation in Detroit. Technicians can also transmit printouts of a customer's automobile directly to Detroit and can receive technical diagrams from Chrysler within minutes.

Further, Galeana's parts department is one of the Southeast's largest, holding $850,000 worth of inventory as compared to the $150,000 worth that most other dealerships carry. Three trucks deliver parts across the state every day, and a new internet web page allows the company to sell parts to locations all over the globe.

### Commitment to Staff

Galeana expects a lot from its staff, and it shows. Their experienced, well-trained employees are different from their counterparts at other dealerships in many ways, most notably in their dedication to the Galeana Automotive Group. It is not uncommon to find Galeana employees celebrating 20 or more years with the company.

Galeana's service technicians attend factory training schools in locations throughout the Southeast. In fact, the dealership recently exceeded Chrysler's dealer training requirement by 800 percent. More than half of them are nationally certified Master Technicians, the highest level a service technician can achieve.

Galeana's sales staff is also expected to meet rigorous training requirements. They take part in two training sessions each week, attend a customer communication training session each year, and take part in Chrysler's product training courses.

∽ Parts Manager John Karaniuk uses electronic parts catalogs to specify the right part.

Further, Galeana offers an apprentice program to students in the Columbia area who choose to major in automobile technology at Midlands Technical College. The dealership pays the costs of tuition, textbooks, and tools as the students work at the dealership part time during the school year and full time during the summer until they graduate and join Galeana full time.

### Commitment to the Community

Cars and trucks aren't, however, the only things Galeana provides to the community. The dealership is very active in local charities like the United Way and the March of Dimes, and they take that commitment to heart.

Each year, Galeana staff members brighten up the holiday season for the kids at Palmetto Place, a shelter for abused children, by donating gifts. They also have provided cars for the March of Dimes Walk America campaign and take part in local education and business initiatives. Galeana is a member of both the Columbia Chamber of Commerce and the Better Business Bureau.

Perhaps the most fun is its work with the Boy Scouts of America, who hold the annual Pinewood Derby in the showroom. Galeana received the 1998 Whitney M. Young Service Award from the Indian Waters Council of Boy Scouts. The showroom is also available to community clubs and schools for their special events.

### Commitment to Excellence

In 1997, Chrysler Corporation and its franchised dealers took a giant leap into the future by redefining the way cars are sold and serviced.

A new "Five Star" performance process certification, quite possibly the most comprehensive in the industry, has been designed to make dealerships displaying the "Five Star" logo the most desirable places to shop.

∽ Chrysler's "Five Star" Certification is proudly noted on the Corporate Brand Sign.

What's the goal? Customer satisfaction! The new "Five Star" program's annual core performance requirements consist of high scores on customer satisfaction and repair quality. Ongoing improvements in sales and service processes are required to be made from information gathered from customers' feedback. Dealers who make the grade earn the right to display the "Five Star" logo.

Daimler-Chrysler Corporation announced back in 1998 that Columbia's Galeana Chrysler-Plymouth-Jeep dealership met all the requirements and can now proudly display the "Five Star" logo. Galeana is the only Chrysler dealership in the Midlands to achieve this tough standard.

The Galena Automotive Group's commitment to its customers, community, and staff will continue to insure its growth as well as the growth of the great communities they reside in, like Columbia! ◉

∽ One of Columbia's finest bodyshops is at Galeana.

# IMIC HOTELS

꙳ **Columbia Sheraton Hotel and Conference Center, Columbia's premier meeting and banquet facility.**

In Columbia, guests have come to know and experience the gracious Southern hospitality that is the signature of Columbia-based IMIC Hotels. It's there in the warm smile of the front desk staff at the Sleep Inn Columbia Northwest, the cheerful greeting from the Sheraton's bellman, and the attentive service demonstrated by the Ramada Plaza's catering staff. Here in Columbia, and at all other IMIC Hotels located throughout the Southeast, the customers' needs are always the priority.

Founded in 1981 By E.L. "Bert" Pooser Jr., Interstate Management and Investment Corporation (IMIC Hotels) manages and/or owns 32 hotels with more than 3,200 guest rooms in South Carolina, North Carolina, Virginia, Tennessee, Georgia, and Florida. With revenues exceeding $75 million, IMIC Hotels ranked 43rd in *Hotels Magazine's* listing of the "Top 100 Management Companies" in the country.

IMIC Hotels employs more than 1,500 people, with more than 400 in Columbia. All IMIC Hotels' employees provide quality service to customers

at the company's various franchises, which include Sheraton Hotels and Conference Centers, Hampton Inns, Quality Suites, Ramada Plaza Hotels, Comfort Suites, Wingate Inns, Sleep Inns, Comfort Inns, Ramada Inns, Suburban Lodges, Days Inns, and the independent Jekyll Island Seafarer Inn and Suites.

In Columbia, IMIC Hotels owns the Columbia Sheraton Hotel and Conference Center off I-20 on Bush River Road, the Sleep Inn Columbia Northwest adjacent to the Sheraton, and the Ramada Plaza Hotel at I-77 and Two Notch Road in northeast Columbia.

꙳ **The Sheraton's "Club Level" offers newly remodeled business class rooms, perfectly equipped to accommodate business after hours yet comfortable enough to provide the most relaxing stay.**

### Sheraton Columbia Hotel and Conference Center

With rows of guest rooms overlooking clusters of palmetto trees in the warmly decorated atrium of the Sheraton, guests feel like they're being welcomed to a tropical resort.

The Columbia Sheraton Hotel and Conference Center has 237 deluxe guest rooms including 34 whirlpool suites that feature microwaves, refrigerators, and wet bars, 3 executive business suites, a presidential suite, a conference suite, and a number of handicapped and nonsmoking rooms. The newly remodeled guest rooms come complete with data ports, full-size irons and ironing boards, salon-style hair dryers, a full selection of toiletries, coffeemakers, and complimentary weekday newspapers. Guests love to unwind in the indoor and outdoor pools and fitness center with sauna and whirlpool.

Guests staying in the upscale club level enjoy an extraordinary level of service. With private access by elevator electronic key, guests are treated to a complimentary deluxe continental breakfast, evening reception in a private lounge, and fluffy terry robes to complete their evening.

The Sheraton boasts the largest conference and banquet center in Columbia with more than 20,000 square feet of meeting and banquet space. The ballroom can accommodate up to 1,800 guests for a reception, and its eight other rooms can be set for corporate meetings, seminars, wedding receptions, bar/bat mitzvahs, and any other special events.

꙳ **The tropical atrium of the Sheraton lends itself to beautiful business luncheons**

Each member of the hotel's sales and convention services staff specializes in meeting planning. From managing a successful corporate meeting to pleasing the mother of the bride, the Sheraton is there to handle every detail in making the event a success.

Andrews Restaurant is well-known for its signature specialties such as honey pecan chicken and filet mignon with tiger shrimp.

General Manager Mark Arnold is proud of the quality of service the Sheraton has become known for. "Our philosophy is very guest focused," he said. "From the greeting you receive at the front desk to the cleanliness of your room, to the quality of the food and other services and amenities, we strive our best every day to put the customer first in all that we do."

### Sleep Inn Columbia Northwest

Adjacent to the Sheraton is the new Sleep Inn Columbia Northwest, also an IMIC Hotel. Offering 78 deluxe guest rooms, whirlpool suites, a fitness center, and meeting room this hotel is built for business and suited for leisure travel. Each guest receives a complimentary deluxe continental breakfast and complimentary *USA Today*. Each guest room is appointed with a large, walk-in shower, iron and ironing board, salon-style hair dryer, data ports, voice mail, and free HBO. Guests staying at the Sleep Inn Columbia Northwest also have unlimited use of the Sheraton's dining, entertainment, and recreational facilities.

### Ramada Plaza Hotel

As the premier full-service hotel in northeast Columbia, the Ramada Plaza Hotel is a mainstay of business travelers, sports enthusiasts, and visiting military to Fort Jackson.

The Ramada Plaza boasts 186 newly remodeled deluxe guest rooms on six floors, including 23 whirlpool suites, a conference suite, and 22 business class rooms. The whirlpool suites include separate sleeping and sitting areas, microwaves, refrigerators, and wet bars. All the deluxe guest rooms are well appointed with data ports, voice mail, two-line telephones with conference-call capabilities, coffeemakers, salon-style hair dryers, full-size irons and ironing boards, and cable television with on-demand movies and games. Many

∽ A work-out in the Ramada Plaza's state-of-the-art fitness center makes for a truly complete stay.

∽ Guests feel the quality and the attention to service the moment they enter the lobby of the Ramada Plaza Hotel.

enjoy a workout in the fully equipped fitness center, complete with sauna, whirlpool, and outdoor pool.

The Ramada Plaza prides itself on quality and service and can put together a luncheon for five or a banquet for 350 in the Hunt Club Ballroom. With full conference services, no detail will be overlooked.

Mallard's Restaurant is popular with the local community for its Southern-style luncheon buffets. Then add the Friday night seafood buffet and Sunday brunch, and you'll see why many make Mallard's a mainstay in their dining options. Mallard's Nightclub, another Columbia favorite, features shag and beach music, a tradition in the Carolinas.

The Ramada Plaza's commitment to guests is evident in the leadership from its general manager, Robert Liptak. Employees say he goes above and

∽ Every event is "special" at Ramada Plaza Hotel.

beyond the call of duty to make sure all of the guests' needs are met. From the cleanliness of the hotel to meeting guests' extra special requests, Liptak's "whatever it takes" philosophy on customer service keeps guests coming back.

### IMIC Hotels on Lake Murray

In addition to the Sheraton, Ramada Plaza, and Sleep Inn, IMIC Hotels owns the Lighthouse Marina and Powerboat Sales and the Rusty Anchor restaurant on Lake Murray. Responding to the needs of the area, the marina has grown to include an award-winning marine sales office, a service dealership, and wet and dry storage for boats. The Rusty Anchor, another award winner, offers lakeside dining in a casual atmosphere. The restaurant features a full menu of seafood, steaks, pasta, and salads. Plus, in warmer months, the adjacent Quarterdeck patio bar offers live entertainment.

And, as it is at all of IMIC's Hotels, guests are treated like royalty, and that's what keeps them coming back time and time again. From the outstanding accommodations to the friendly, personal service, IMIC Hotels is "Proving Southern Hospitality Still Exists." ◨

# ADAM'S MARK HOTEL COLUMBIA

A first-class hotel should be much more than a source of fine accommodations—it should also serve as a valuable community resource.

So says James Gibson, general manager of the Adam's Mark Hotel Columbia, adding that the dedication of his 180-plus staff, coupled with the hotel's flexible space and ideal location, help create memorable "get-together" opportunities for guests as diverse as business leaders and prospective brides.

For business leaders who are looking for flexible facilities that feature convenience and sophistication, the Adam's Mark Columbia offers more than 26,000 square feet of meeting space—more than 10,000 square feet of prefunction space and 15 individual meeting rooms—and complete audio-visual capabilities and technicians.

More than 300 luxurious rooms and suites extend that attention to convenience, with each room featuring oversized work desks, phones with voice mail and data ports, and other amenities geared to the professional. And for "down time," opportunities abound for all guests to unwind from a long day of meetings with an indoor heated pool, outdoor sundeck, and fully equipped health club within the facility.

Equal consideration is given to those seeking grandeur and convenience in sites for weddings, holiday parties, or other festive occasions. The Adam's Mark Columbia has three ballrooms and a 10,000-square-foot atrium—enough space to accommodate 850 people. The hotel's catering services guarantee highly individualized menus, everything from hot dogs with chili and lemon meringue pie to Chicken Montmorency and chocolate-dipped cheesecake with mango puree.

The Adam's Mark Columbia served as host to countless catered events last year, ranging from large groups to small company parties, Gibson says.

"People tend to look at us as a gathering place for important times in their lives. We are honored that they allow us to play such a role in the creation of these treasured memories," Gibson says.

↶ A first-class hotel should be much more than a source of fine accommodations—it should also serve as a valuable community resource. Adam's Mark Hotel Columbia, with its dedicated 180-plus staff, flexible space, and ideal location, helps create memorable "get-together" opportunities.

Located just nine miles from Columbia Metropolitan Airport and a few blocks from the State Capitol, the Columbia Museum of Art, and the University of South Carolina campus, the Adam's Mark Columbia could not have a more convenient downtown location for the business leader or wedding party.

However, Gibson is quick to assert that the Adam's Mark Columbia has just as much to offer the Columbia-area resident who is looking for a gathering place to meet friends or enjoy a quiet dinner. Indeed, Adam's Mark officials attest that some of the best entertainment and dining in Adam's Mark cities can be found at these hotels.

Which brings up the question of what Columbia-area hotel is known for "Columbia's Best Sunday Brunch"? You guessed it: Adam's Mark Columbia.

And drive by the hotel on a fall weekday lunch hour and you may hear strains of jazz, as musicians play to outdoor diners. Stroll by Players, the Adam's Mark Columbia's sports bar, during a University of South Carolina basketball game and you may hear the sounds of die-hard fans watching large-screen TVs and cheering the home team to victory.

Other amenities include Finlay's American Restaurant—with the city's most imaginative buffet and pasta bar—and the Tiffany Rose Lounge, regularly featuring live entertainment.

"We cater to large groups and functions regularly, but are equally dedicated to attracting smaller groups," says Gibson. "Each group, no matter how large, receives the best quality of service we can offer." ◪

↶ The Adam's Mark's Tiffany Rose Lounge regularly features live entertainment.

# WOODCREEK FARMS AND THE COUNTRY CLUB

### Woodcreek Farms

Woodcreek Farms—Columbia's finest Country Club Community presenting a premier venue for homes of elegance and distinction. Located in Northeast Richland County just off the I-20 Pontiac exit, Woodcreek Farms combines all the convenience of living minutes away from town, with the quiet, natural setting of the country.

Whether it's a round of golf on its Tom Fazio masterpiece or a stroll along the nature trails, residents will be greeted by pristine lakes and ponds and tracts of hardwoods, wetlands, and wild flowers. Woodcreek Farms melds all the beauty and recreation that nature and man can offer.

From the Courtyard Homes nestled within a short walk to The Country Club to executive golf-course and lake-front properties, a variety of lifestyle choices awaits you at Woodcreek Farms. Live leisurely—dwell graciously in a community of unmatched beauty, outstanding amenities, and an incomparable commitment to excellence.

### The Country Club at WildeWood and Woodcreek Farms

It's not the active social calendar, tennis, swimming pools, or the natural beauty that makes The Country Club at WildeWood and Woodcreek Farms incomparable in Columbia. It's not even the spectacular golf courses, designed by two of the sport's most accomplished architects. It's the staff, the club members, their families and friends, and the commitment to providing the ultimate in service and amenities that make the difference.

Other communities can boast of the privilege and reward of membership in their Club, but there is something better—a unique advantage offered only by The Country Club at WildeWood and Woodcreek Farms. When you become a member, there are two levels of participation: access to WildeWood only or access to both WildeWood and Woodcreek Farms. WildeWood celebrated its 25th anniversary recently. Woodcreek Farms opened fall of 1997, thereby offering two levels of participation. That means 2 exceptional facilities, 14 tennis courts, Olympic-class swimming, and 2 prestigious golf courses.

Speaking of golf, WildeWood's 6,724-yard, 18-hole, par-72 championship course, designed by master architect Russell Breeden, is designed to provide a challenging experience to golfers of all levels. Four sets of tees, no parallel fairways, and varying elevations over the course's 130 acres are evidence of the club's commitment to deliver the most rewarding golf experience with every round.

Woodcreek Farms' challenging 18-hole, 7,002-yard, par-72 championship course, designed by world-renowned architect Tom Fazio, is molded to the unique midlands environment and topography. It winds through pecan groves, wild flowers, natural streams and lakes, and even a waterfall. As you drive the course, you will experience the presence of nature itself, creating a tranquility

∽ The Island green of the 15th hole offers a tranquil view to Northwoods Lake residents while challenging the best golfers.

that allows you to concentrate on your game, enjoy the company of friends, and play the game the way it was meant to be played.

With indoor, climate-controlled tennis courts and stadium courts available at WildeWood and Woodcreek Farms, tennis is always in season. A variety of events and instructional programs are planned for both juniors and adults throughout the year. Youth activities including day camps during the summer months are also provided. The adult calendar consists of dining, dancing, bridge, theme parties, and numerous tournaments for tennis and golf. Coupled with social activities, lasting relationships are forged and new friendships are nourished by The Country Club's commitment to provide a warm environment for social camaraderie. **C**

∽ While every home at Woodcreek Farms must adhere to stringent architectural guidelines, each is as unique as the family who lives there.

# Chapter 11

## Networks

Photo by Suzanne McGrane

# COLUMBIA METROPOLITAN AIRPORT

Known as the front door to the Columbia community, Columbia Metropolitan Airport holds a warm welcome sign for travelers who fly into Columbia. Located six miles southwest of Columbia's central business district and conveniently located near interstate highways that are centered in Columbia—I-20, I-26, and I-77—the airport is much like a 2,600-acre city with more than 50 agencies and businesses located on the airport property. The Columbia Metropolitan terminal complex serves more than a million passengers annually, and United Parcel Service opened a Southeastern Regional Freight Hub at the airport in August 1996. The hub includes a 330,000-square-foot package sorting facility and a 41,000-square-foot general purpose building.

Whether they are on business, visiting family, or coming home, travelers who walk off their plane and into the recently renovated, magnificent airport will marvel at its beauty. The blue glass, elevated skylights, and blue and silver custom carpet carefully carry passengers from their plane seats to baggage claim. And all along the way, travelers will enjoy the friendly customer service they will receive while they are at the airport.

⤳ **The Airport provides a welcome front door to the community.**

After all, Columbia Metropolitan Airport prides itself on its "can-do" attitude.

"Our buzz word here is accommodation," said Lynne Douglas, director of marketing for Columbia Metropolitan Airport. "Whatever we can do to accommodate our customers, we do. We strive to serve the needs of the traveling public and to be as accommodating to those needs as possible."

One of the ways Columbia Metropolitan Airport has met the needs of the traveling public is by renovating the airport. A $50-million, two-year airport renovation project was completed in 1997. The project included a new two-level concourse, which opened in October 1996. The new concourse has common-use gates that accommodate more passengers and a wider variety of aircraft types and sizes. The new food court lets hungry travelers enjoy a delicious bite to eat before beginning their journey, while the Paradies Airport Shop welcomes travelers in search of South Carolina souvenirs, good reading materials, or a quick snack to take on the plane.

The connector leading from the main terminal to the new concourse is 280 feet long and includes moving sidewalks. These sidewalks are the first in South Carolina. The second phase of the project included a complete renovation of the existing terminal building. This included expansion of airline ticket counter areas, baggage claim, and airline baggage make-up areas. New interior and exterior architectural features and finishes have been added to include tinted glass and pyramid skylights. In addition, modifications throughout the terminal and parking lot were designed to accommodate the mobility impaired and comply with the Americans with Disabilities Act.

Douglas said the most rewarding aspect of being a part of the airport staff was the renovation project.

"Seeing all the wonderful changes the airport has been through has been very rewarding," she said. "It's like seeing a caterpillar turning into a butterfly. It's been a great time to see the fruits of our labor come to fruition."

The "fruits" she is referring to are an increase in airline partners in recent years, which translates into more nonstop destinations and better choices for the traveling public. United Parcel Service's selection of the

⤳ **A $50-million renovation project was completed in 1997.**

<cx> The Airport is a major player in the economic development of the area.

airport as its major Southeast freight hub has resulted in an increase in air cargo in recent years. In addition, Columbia Metropolitan Airport remains in constant communication with potential new airlines.

Douglas said the airport actively pursues these relationships to assist with the economic development of the Midlands and the state. In addition, if it can help attract more visitors and potential businesses to Columbia by offering a warm welcome, the airport feels it is giving back to its community.

"We have an opportunity to assist people, and knowing that you made their traveling experience much better than they probably thought it would be is very fulfilling," Douglas said.

And that's why Columbia Metropolitan Airport is the perfect doorway into this community. ▣

<cx> Unique landscaping features provide a tranquil setting for travelers.

171

# SCANA CORPORATION

SCANA Corporation has a 150-plus year history of providing reliable and affordable energy to its customers. From its beginnings in 1846 as the Charleston Gas Light Company, SCANA has evolved into a Southeastern focused corporation that is expanding outside of its traditional utility role to provide customers with additional services from telecommunications to home security.

"We're changing the way our customers think of their power company," says William (Bill) Timmerman, SCANA chairman, president, and CEO. "From providing energy for cooking and heating in our traditional marketplace, to expanding into the telecommunications business in 13 states, we're building on a strong foundation to provide even more services to our customers."

SCANA's principal subsidiary, South Carolina Electric & Gas Company (SCE&G), is the state's largest utility, supplying electric service to more than 520,000 customers in the central, southern, and southwestern portions of the state. SCE&G is the state's largest retail supplier of natural gas as well, with more than 264,000 customers throughout a 19,000-square-mile service area.

SCANA has also made considerable strides in growth in other states. In 1998, SCANA Energy was formed and began marketing gas to residential, commercial, and industrial customers in the deregulated Georgia gas market. SCANA Energy's focus and creativity helped the company become a dominant player in the natural gas residential market, acquiring more than 425,000 customers.

In 1999, SCANA again grew its gas interest and announced it was acquiring Public Service Natural Gas (PSNC) of Gastonia, North Carolina. PSNC Energy officially joined the SCANA family on February 10, 2000, bringing with it a natural gas distribution system with over 344,000 customers in a 31-county service territory.

In addition to being a major natural gas and electricity provider, SCANA companies provide services beyond the traditional utility meter. The ServiceCare appliance protection program, coupled with SCANA Security systems, is providing customers with peace of mind at home or in their business.

Other subsidiaries in the SCANA family of energy-related businesses extend beyond South Carolina. The company markets and transports natural gas. And in addition to its power plant management and maintenance services, SCANA is a leader in fiber-optic telecommunications, with 2,500 miles of fiber installed or under construction throughout the Southeast. SCANA's 800mhz system serves as the communications backbone for some 8,200 emergency service subscribers throughout South Carolina, providing a reliable source of communications during emergency situations.

SCANA Communications provides fiber-optic telecommunications and video conferencing services in South Carolina. The company also has investments in Powertel, one of the fastest growing wireless personal communication services (PCS) providers in the Southeast; ITC DeltaCom, a fully integrated telecommunications company providing local and long-distance telephone service, data services, Internet access, and other services; and Knology Holdings, Inc., a multifunctional telecommunications company offering expanded cable television, telephone service, and Internet access.

Along with focusing on meeting customer needs, SCANA is focused on making South Carolina successful. More and more, companies are discovering that South Carolina is the location that meets their needs for future growth in an increasingly competitive global market. And one of the best ways to obtain access to

☙ **SCE&G linemen are known for their quick response and restoration expertise.** *Photo by Brian Dressler*

decade—programs that challenge youth, recognize academic success, and provide appropriate environments for learning. On the corporate level, they've provided support through people, money, and leadership in programs such as Communities in Schools and Junior Achievement. And wherever you go throughout their service area, you'll find their employees serving on educational boards and volunteering their time to improve South Carolina's educational resources. From teaching children good study habits at its 20 South Carolina Homework Centers to supporting the Communities in Schools program, SCANA is helping students discover their potential for learning.

And SCE&G's customer assistance program helps elderly, handicapped, and low-income residents obtain financial aid from local, state, and federal agencies. The company's Good Neighbor Fund allows individual SCANA employees to authorize payroll deductions to help provide emergency aid to families in need.

"While we are very customer-focused, we are also very community-focused," says Timmerman. "As partners in the growth and progress of our state, we are committed to making our communities better places in every way we can. We're proud to do business in South Carolina." G

∽ **SCANA has a long history of commitment to education, as was illustrated through the donation of $500,000 towards Governor Hodges First Steps program, as pictured above.**

resources in South Carolina is through the SCANA Community/Economic Development and Local Government Department. As a major proponent of economic development in South Carolina, SCANA integrates its corporate resources into the needs of the communities it serves. Since the early 1960s, SCE&G's Economic Development Department has worked on marketing and industrial recruiting efforts and assisted with the recruitment of such corporations as Caterpillar in Sumter County, Bridgestone/Firestone in Aiken County, and Bayer, CIGNA, and Dynapower/Stratopower in the Lowcountry.

In addition, SCANA created a Community Development Grant Program and a Revolving Loan Program in 1990. These programs provide essential capital to help South Carolina communities build infrastructure improvements required by business and industry. They provide leverage for municipal and county governments, sometimes tripling available funds. New and expanding business and industry translates into more jobs and a broader tax base, which improves the quality of life throughout South Carolina. From 1990 to 1999, SCANA's grants and loans programs contributed nearly $5.5 million and has helped retain or attract more than 22,000 new jobs to the company's service area.

Through a long list of corporate programs, SCANA has continued to demonstrate a strong commitment to enhancing the overall quality of life in South Carolina. An investment in education is an investment in the future. That's why SCANA and its family of businesses have been initiating, sponsoring, and supporting education programs throughout the state for more than a

∽ **SCE&G provides natural gas service to over 264,000 customers throughout its service territory.**

# BELLSOUTH

Rotary phones to touch-tone to answering machines to paging devices to cellular phones to wireless to the World Wide Web to ADSL. The technology is constantly evolving, but the mission at BellSouth hasn't changed in more than 100 years: to provide the best, most innovative telecommunication services available to customers in South Carolina.

BellSouth is a $25-billion communications services company. It provides telecommunications, wireless and wireless long distance communications, video and entertainment services, advertising and publishing, and Internet and data services to more than nearly 37 million customers in 20 countries worldwide and in 9 southeastern states, including South Carolina.

"Our customers in South Carolina and throughout the world depend on BellSouth for communications, especially during times of crises such as hurricanes," said Martha Smith, BellSouth Midlands regional director. "We cannot promise that no customer will lose service during a natural disaster, but we do have the products and services available to help customers develop contingency plans in case a disaster strikes. We can guarantee that BellSouth will be prepared."

And BellSouth guarantees its business and residential customers that it is prepared for the future—a new century in which dazzling technological innovations will create countless options in the telecommunications industry that will increase freedom and flexibility. BellSouth's operations, serving 66 percent of the state's telephone customers, have made the commitment to lead the way toward that future. Following are some examples of BellSouth's level of commitment to South Carolina.

↪ **Joe Anderson, President of BellSouth in South Carolina.**

Since 1994, BellSouth has invested $1 billion in South Carolina, including $234 million in 1999.

BellSouth has more than $2.6 billion in assets to support 138,300 miles of fiber-optic cable.

More than 3,500 employees serve over 1.4 million access lines and 84 local calling exchanges, including 45 percent of the state's geography and 36 of its counties.

For four consecutive years, BellSouth has captured the highest ranking in the J.D. Power and Associates Local Residential Telephone Service Satisfaction Study℠.

High-speed connections to the Internet, web-based e-mail, text messaging (via phone or computer)—BellSouth is meeting the needs of today's fast-paced South Carolinian, and at the most affordable costs. Basic rates in South Carolina have not increased since 1985.

Another way BellSouth demonstrates its commitment to its South Carolina customers, and its investment in this state, is through its community and education initiatives.

In its 11th year, BellSouth publishes the South Carolina African-American History Calendar, which focuses on social studies curriculum. The calendar is given to school districts to distribute to all teachers throughout South Carolina.

Another example is BellSouth's commitment to making sure that all students have access to the World Wide Web. In South Carolina BellSouth invested over $2 million, touched over 500 schools, provided over 350 wiring kits to wire schools for the Internet, offered free Internet access for teachers for nine months, and awarded approximately $60,000 in grants.

South Carolina is one of four states in the nation to have every K-12 school connected to the Internet. Also, the BellSouth Foundation, which is committed to fostering improved K-12 education, has granted almost $3 million to schools and programs in South Carolina.

"We feel so honored to serve so many of our state's businesses and residents," says Smith. "They have put their trust in us, and we are going to make sure that we earn that trust and express our appreciation every single day." ☙

↪ **BellSouth is Y-2 ready.**

# TIME WARNER CABLE

Time Warner Cable is bringing Columbia into an exciting new era in home entertainment and information. The company's substantial investment in fiber-optic system upgrades and new digital technology enables its subscribers to receive more and better programming, enhanced picture and sound quality, improved signal reliability, and advanced telecommunications products and services. These products and services include new cable networks, multiplexed premium channels, more local programming and local broadcast stations, and new digital program tiers and pay-per-view options.

Another exciting new service available to Columbia residents is Road Runner, a high-speed, on-line Internet access service provided via cable modems. "With the arrival of Digital Cable and Road Runner, Time Warner Cable continues to be the leader in the cable television industry," says Sam Nalbone, vice president and general manager. "These new cable services will enable our company to better serve the people of the greater Columbia area."

Time Warner Cable is committed to providing its customers the best service possible. Nalbone added, "We are committed to outstanding customer service not just because it's a good business investment, but because it's the right thing to do."

Time Warner Cable employees are the company's most valuable resource in today's competitive communications environment. The company has more than 300 employees in the Midlands. Customer service and sales representatives handle more than 75,000 calls each month, answering over 90 percent in 30 seconds or less, while maintenance technicians respond to area outages on an average of less than one hour.

Time Warner Cable believes that corporate citizens play a large role in the success of a community. That's why the company and its employees are very active in numerous civic and charitable organizations in Columbia, supporting everything from the arts and health organizations to crime prevention and youth sports.

Time Warner Cable is also committed to education. Through its support of the Cable in the Classroom initiative, the company provides complimentary cable service to local schools and over 540 hours of high-quality,

☞ **Road Runner, a high-speed, on-line Internet access service provided via cable modems, is an exciting new service to Columbia residents.**

commercial-free educational programming each month. Time Warner Cable also provides a monthly programming guide, workshops, lesson plans, and other educational resources to area schools, all free of charge. Time Warner Cable actively participates in the Family and Community Critical Viewing Project by offering "Taking Charge of Your TV" workshops for parents, educators, and community organizations to increase awareness and understanding of critical viewing techniques and media literacy skills.

Time Warner Cable has grown steadily since its entry into the greater Columbia market in 1996, today serving more than 131,000 customers in 24 communities throughout the area. Customers enjoy more than 50,000 hours of programming each month on 77 channels—including favorites ESPN, HBO, Discovery Channel, A&E, The History Channel, Lifetime Television, and American Movie Classics—delivered by more than 2,400 miles of distribution plant. Digital cable subscribers enjoy even more channels and programming choices, including more first-run movies, 40 channels of Music Choice, and 38 channels of Pay-Per-View.

Time Warner Cable: Imagine what's next. ☒

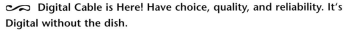

☞ **Digital Cable is Here! Have choice, quality, and reliability. It's Digital without the dish.**

Photo by Suzanne McGrane

# Chapter 12

# Distribution, Manufacturing & Technology

*Photo by Suzanne McGrane*

# USC College of Engineering & Information Technology Launches USC's High Technology Incubator

While it may seem unusual to have an economic development office in an engineering school, officials from the University of South Carolina's College of Engineering & Information Technology think it makes perfect sense. After all, the economy of this region depends on innovations in research and development. And the College firmly believes in establishing strong foundations for new business growth and quality education in technical fields for the future generations of Columbia's workforce.

Dr. Michael Reischman, associate dean of the College of Engineering & Information Technology, says South Carolina's economy is experiencing rapid growth, especially in attracting high-tech industry. "We need to be responsive and in tune with where the state is going," he said. "That way, we can train our students for professional engineering careers and contribute to research and development projects that will benefit the entire state."

College leaders believe that expanding the state's high-tech businesses will boost the state's economy and result in higher incomes for its residents. South Carolina currently ranks 26th in the country in the percentage of high-tech establishments. And while high-tech companies represent less than one percent of all business establishments, their annual payrolls have a big impact. High-tech industry accounts for 4.1 percent of the state's total payroll, ranking South Carolina 14th in the nation. The College is fast becoming a national model for educational institutions through its dedication to economic development. The Southeast is filled with opportunities for business and industry. By making economic development a priority at the University, the College hopes to play a vital role in future business endeavors.

### Help for Entrepreneurs

Two electrical engineers at a local computer company have an idea about creating a new business. They know all the technical aspects to make their idea work, but need help with business development. They could also use some legal advice, human resources management, and access to office and laboratory equipment. They are excellent candidates for USC's new high-tech incubation program managed by the South Carolina Research Institute (SCRI). Just like real incubators are used to maintain favorable environmental conditions to nurture development, this high-tech incubator is designed to foster development of emerging companies and ideas. Joel Stevenson, director of the USC Columbia Technology Incubator, has brought his business expertise to help nurture these emerging companies through their vulnerable start-up phases.

"Statistics show that 80 percent of new businesses fail in a traditional start-up environment," Stevenson said. "The risk is greatly reduced through an incubation program."

Companies that are admitted into the program fulfill several requirements. The product or service needs to be technology based and have the potential

In addition to working with incubating companies, undergraduate students have the opportunity to work on research teams such as this pilot plant scale of the Savannah River site filters. Here students work with FRED (Filtration Research Engineering Demonstration) to test cross-flow filters that operate following ISO-9000 guidelines. The students evaluate how efficiently non-radioactive simulants of nuclear waste can be treated.

to reach significant revenue levels, allowing the company to graduate from the incubator program in approximately two to three years. The company should have substantial interaction with the University R&D enterprise and have the potential to create new jobs that contribute to South Carolina's economic development.

And finally, entrepreneurs should have the education and experience needed in the appropriate technical field and be willing to accept guidance and share management responsibility with others to make the company successful. With a business plan in hand, these companies are helping to promote, stimulate, and support economic development in the Columbia region and beyond.

### A Full House

After less than a year in existence, the SCRI's incubator program can already take claim to an entrepreneurial success story. KryoTech, a manufacturing company that produces a product that cools computer chips to make them run faster, spent time in the College's incubator program before launching its own facility in West Columbia. KryoTech began with six engineers from NCR housed in the 3,000-square-foot incubator and has grown to more than 50 employees, a dozen of whom have USC degrees, in a space triple the size of their start-up facility.

Not only was KryoTech able to use several students from the College to assist with the project, but the company also was able to tap into the expertise of a number of professors who specialize in thermal engineering. There are currently three companies located in the incubator. E811, Inc. is a faculty-owned company that was started by physics professor Joe Johnson. The company provides data warehousing and analysis for legal and health-care clients, while also developing software products and offering other services. Correlated Solutions, Inc. is another faculty-owned business. Two mechanical engineering professors have created a computer imaging system for use in Department of Energy and NASA labs. Finally, NetGen Learning Systems is a company working on technology-enabled learning products for professional development and certification of technology professionals.

### Heading in the Same Direction

One of the most important ingredients in a successful university incubation program is the development of important partnerships, including establishing working relationships with other colleges on campus, state and government leaders, and the business and professional communities.

USC's College of Engineering & Information Technology, the founders of the incubator program, knew that these relationships were an integral part of making the incubator work, and so it focused on developing ties with various groups and organizations before the incubator was launched. These groups include the Central Carolina Economic Development Alliance, the City of Columbia, Lexington County, Richland County, South Carolina Electric and Gas, South Carolina Technology Alliance, South Carolina Department of Commerce, Tomlin and Company, the USC Darla Moore School of Business, and the USC College of Science and Math.

cx/⌒ **Structural engineer Dr. Michael Petrou works with his students to test the use of glass fiber reinforced polymer composites to rehabilitate aging concrete. Tests such as these and others allow engineers to determine the strength of aging structures and how to fortify them for continued usage. Engineering faculty and students are valuable resources to incubating companies, and many students find employment with these companies upon graduation.**

It also is working closely with the South Carolina Research Authority to match economic development activities with College of Engineering & Information Technology resources. The Research Authority is already collaborating with the College on projects that will bring additional industrial research contracts to the state. In turn, the Research Authority also is inviting its customers to have broader access to universities and their educational products.

While the College of Engineering & Information Technology is educating engineers, it is also helping to create jobs for students when they graduate by forming these economic development partnerships. By cooperating with business, government, and educational leaders, the College is establishing the roots of relationships that will build South Carolina's future.

### The Next Century

The technology incubation program at USC is still in its initial growth phase, with plans to acquire space for new companies as the project expands. The initial incubator is located at the USC College of Engineering & Information Technology, but future plans are to utilize sites in downtown Columbia near the campus.

Within five years, leaders at the College hope to attract even more companies to be a part of the incubator project in a larger, 60,000-square-foot facility located on campus.

And as the College of Engineering & Information Technology recruits, builds, and deploys new technology-driven companies to support South Carolina's knowledge-based industry, the economic development in the state will continue to grow to create an abundance of wealth and opportunities. ⧉

# UNITED PARCEL SERVICE

*South Carolina District Manger Mike Brock.* Photo by Mike Hawkin

During the early morning hours when most Columbians are in the middle of a good night's sleep, hundreds of people fill a 350,000-square-foot building adjacent to the Columbia Metropolitan Airport to use the most efficient cutting-edge technology to sort and route hundreds of thousands of packages, letters, and documents bound for destinations throughout the Southeast. This is UPS, the world's largest package distribution company that handles more than 3 billion parcels each year throughout the world.

The UPS Columbia Air Hub—a $40-million, 68-acre facility that opened in August 1996—is capable of sorting 42,000 packages per hour and is served by 16 daily jet aircraft flights, half of which arrive between 11 P.M. and 1 A.M. and are unloaded, sorted, and rerouted by 3 A.M. Whispering into the night sky, the same eight jets launch out between 3:15 and 3:45 almost every morning carrying packages that will need to be loaded into package cars and delivered to customers that same morning.

Precise timing is what guides the company and what has led to its success in the competitive parcel delivery industry. UPS South Carolina District Manager Mike Brock said, "UPS has quickly become a prime example of the Midlands' emphasis on high-tech business solutions.

"The technology used by UPS is incredible: from specially designed package-delivery vehicles including a fleet of 224 highly sophisticated aircraft, to UPSnet, a global electronic data communications network that provides an information pipeline for international package processing and delivery, our company is certainly on the cutting edge of all industries," Brock said.

With more than 500,000 miles of communication lines and its own satellite,

UPSnet links more than 1,300 distribution sites in 46 countries and tracks millions of packages daily. The investment UPS has put into technology in the past five years is in the billions. As the evolution of electronic commerce unfolds, UPS's "reason for being" is to enable global commerce. "Our goal is to serve the dynamic distribution, logistics, and commerce needs of our customers worldwide, integrating the physical and virtual worlds of business transactions," said District Sales Manager Nola Wood.

And there's more to come, with Columbia among the beneficiaries. By 2005, employment at the Columbia Air Hub and Ground Hub facilities is expected to reach over 1,900.

### Rich in History

UPS can trace its beginnings to a neighborhood package delivery service started more than 90 years ago. It was 1907, and it would be another six years before the U.S. Postal Service would begin its parcel post system. An enterprising 19-year-old, James E. (Jim) Casey, stepped forward to deliver a solution to America's growing parcel delivery needs. With $100 he borrowed from a friend, Casey established the American Messenger Company in Seattle, Washington, where Jim and a handful of other teenagers, including his brother George, began delivering packages for local retailers.

That was the birth of United Parcel Service, and Jim Casey's motto— "Best Service and Lowest Rates"—still guides UPS today.

From the beginning, Casey made sure that his messengers were on time, clean, and friendly. Even today, neatly uniformed and friendly service providers remain a company standard. First making deliveries by foot, on streetcars, and bicycles, the company grew to a new fleet of delivery vehicles when Casey partnered with Charles Soderstrom in 1913 to create Merchants Parcel Delivery. It was Soderstrom who decided to institute the rich Pullman brown color on the company's new Model-T Fords, a color that is still used

The UPS/United Way Tug-A-Plane event is held annually at the UPS Columbia Air Ramp. To raise money for the United Way of the Midlands, UPS invites community members to enter a team to compete for the lowest tug time. Each team pulls a 727 airplane 25 feet. Offering food from local vendors and Kiddie tug-a-plane, the event hosts fun for the entire family.

〜 **Cal Darden, UPS senior vice president of operations, served as the 1998 keynote speaker for the Columbia Urban League's Equal Opportunity Day Dinner. Pictured left to right: J.T. McLawhorn, Mike Brock, and Cal Darden.**

on the 900 package cars running pick up and delivery service from 17 ground centers around South Carolina today. UPS began serving the Palmetto State in 1967.

### Company Operations

Today, Columbia is home to one of the company's six U.S. Regional Express Hubs, which together with the main hub in Louisville, Kentucky, make it possible for UPS to deliver more than 12.4 million packages and documents around the world every day.

The UPS network of hubs is the key to its success. And Columbia is a key hub in the network, providing an efficient link between the southeastern United States and Chicago and New York City. Every afternoon, thousands of packages from local operating centers make their way by truck to Columbia, where they're carefully unloaded.

In an extremely fast-paced operation, the packages are sorted by ZIP code, tracked by bar code, and consolidated onto conveyor belts that move them nonstop to the other end of the hub. There, the packages are put through a second, more detailed sorting process and routed to an out-bound trailer, to a package car serving the immediate area, or, for packages with a more distant destination, to a UPS jet.

### Community Involvement

When it comes to Columbia and the other 1,492 communities around the country UPS calls home, the company delivers more than parcels, packages, and documents. Whether it's supplying disadvantaged youth with quality sports equipment through the UPS Olympic Sports Legacy Program or teaching thousands of parents job skills through the company's Family and Workplace Literacy Initiative, UPS is committed to investing in the communities where its employees and customers live and work.

Guided by the philosophy of its founder, Jim Casey, who said, "You can't truly understand someone's problems unless you walk in their shoes," UPS employees are strongly encouraged to get involved in community service activities. Through its local Neighbor to Neighbor program, UPS employees donate countless hours to organizations such as Habitat for Humanity, Palmetto Health Alliance First Ladies' Walk for Life, Harvest Hope Food Bank, the local chapter of the American Red Cross, United Way, City Year Columbia, and Special Olympics.

UPS's partnership with the Columbia Urban League supports programs like Welfare to Work, which helps connect local welfare recipients with employment opportunities; School to Work, which works with Columbia's youth to prepare them to enter the labor force; and the Black Executive Exchange Program, which helps entrepreneurs fulfill their dreams.

Both on a local level and globally, the "UPS Charter" includes building on its legacy as a caring and responsible corporate citizen, often using its worldwide transportation infrastructure to ensure the delivery of goods to more than 200 countries around the world.

When it comes to serving customers in South Carolina or the entire global community, you can count on UPS to deliver the total package. 🅖

〜 **UPS at Columbia Chamber of Commerce.**

# WESTINGHOUSE NUCLEAR FUEL BUSINESS UNIT

Since 1969, Westinghouse Electric Company has played a large role in meeting the nation's energy needs. Westinghouse Electric Company's Nuclear Fuel Business Unit (NFBU), Columbia Site—the largest facility of its kind in the world—provides fuel and other products used to generate nearly 10 percent of America's electricity. In fact, the fuel and fuel-related products produced at the Columbia Plant are used in countries worldwide, including Belgium, Brazil, Czech Republic, France, Japan, Slovenia, South Korea, Spain, Sweden, Taiwan, and the United Kingdom.

The Columbia complex covers 1,155 acres and includes 550,000 square feet of manufacturing and office space, employing about 900 personnel with an annual payroll of more than $53 million.

However, quantity isn't the truest measure of the work performed at Westinghouse—safety and quality are just as, if not more, important.

"A commitment to safety is our plant's top priority, and we have a record to be proud of. We've operated for more than 60-million man-hours—30 years—without a serious nuclear exposure or impact on the public or the environment," says Columbia Site Plant Manager Jack Allen.

Westinghouse is one of the original members of the National Safety Council, and the Columbia facility continuously meets and often exceeds all regulatory requirements for waste management and reduction.

Employees build the components that make a finished fuel assembly for use in commercial nuclear reactors, as well as various reactor core components such as control rods, source rods, plugging devices, and burnable absorber assemblies. This work demands the highest quality, and Westinghouse delivers.

"In 1988, we were presented with one of the first three Malcolm Baldridge National Quality Awards ever given," Allen says. The award was presented by the president of the United States in recognition of excellence in quality management.

*Proud To Be A Part of the Midlands.* **The 1,155-acre, 900-personnel Westinghouse Nuclear Fuel Business Unit Columbia Site has safely and responsibly manufactured commercial nuclear fuel at its Bluff Road site since 1969. It looks forward to continuing to help shape the economic and business climate of the Midlands, to aid in guiding the area's growth and evolution, and to lend a leading hand in solving community social ills and problems.**

*We don't look good, if you don't look good.* **As a part of the Midlands area community family, Westinghouse takes seriously its responsibility to aid those in need. More than $150,000 is donated annually, by both employees and the company, to area charities. Additionally, employees are encouraged to individually and collectively donate their time and talents to community service organizations supported by Westinghouse—like Habitat for Humanity—as well as others of their choosing. An award is presented annually to the employee exhibiting the most outstanding community service participation.**

In 1992, the Commercial Nuclear Fuel Division (expanded and renamed the NFBU) became the first recipient of the "Chairman's Gold Award" in the George Westinghouse Total Quality Awards program, the highest honor awarded by Westinghouse for excellence in quality improvement.

Even with its global importance and reputation, the Columbia Site is deeply committed to its home community. In 1999, over $50,000 was donated by the company to local charities such as the Juvenile Diabetes Foundation, the March of Dimes, United Way, and Junior Achievement. In 1998, Westinghouse Columbia Site agreed to provide a $10,000 grant to the Palmetto Emergency Shelter to aid in providing a much-needed safe haven for children subjected to domestic violence, abuse, and neglect. Individual employees also donate their time and talents to a number of community service organizations such as Habitat for Humanity and Junior Achievement.

"We take as much pride in serving our community as we do in our work," says Allen. And for more than 30 years, Westinghouse has served the world from Columbia. ◖

# CATE-MCLAURIN COMPANY

Character. Quality. Community. What do these three things have in common? They're the foundation of Cate-McLaurin Company, a commercial tire service firm located at 1001 Idlewild Boulevard. With a service area that encompasses a 120-mile radius from Columbia, it effectively serves most of the Palmetto State.

Cate-McLaurin began operations in 1932 as McMaster and Cate Tire Co. bearing the names of cofounders Charles J. Cate Jr. and Samuel Buchanan McMaster—two men of strong character who would drive its early success. The company was originally an addition to S.B. McMaster Co., a local sporting goods store, and in the early days changed tires on the sidewalk at the corner of Sumter and Hampton Streets in Columbia. McMaster financed the business, while Charlie Cate supplied the "sweat equity."

Around 1935, J.W. McLaurin came on board as a wholesale manager. Hailing from North Carolina, he was able to develop accounts as far north

as Laurinburg. With the death of McMaster, Cate and McLaurin purchased the McMaster interest and began a process that would change its name and face, and introduce a broadened line of high-quality products.

By the end of 1938, the business had grown to include electrical appliances, further expanding in the late 1940s and '50s with "brown goods"—including a magical new technology called television—along with tires and hardware. Certainly the arrival of, and demand for, TV drove some of the change in goods. But World War II was also a factor. Because of a shortage of goods brought on by the war, Cate-McLaurin found itself selling a wider variety of products—sporting goods, hardware, toys, and just about anything else customers needed. It was during WWII that the company began retreading tires.

As the years passed, competition from other product lines and larger manufacturers brought the company back to a core business of televisions and appliances—and, of course, the tire business. In 1971, Cate-McLaurin purchased A&M Tire on Rosewood Drive, an acquisition that also brought the Bandag retread franchise, and the Michelin and Bridgestone tire lines.

Business was so good that within two years, the company had outgrown its Rosewood Drive location, and construction began on the Idlewild Boulevard facility.

By the late 1980s, Cate-McLaurin decided to leave the television and appliance lines altogether, focusing on its high-growth, highly successful commercial truck tire business. Today, under the leadership of brothers William and Charles Cate and their sons Walker and Perry, along with Vice Presidents Frank Clayton, Scott McPherson, and Jim Wadford, the company has maintained that focus. Forty-five percent of its business centers on Bandag retreading, 45 percent on new truck tire sales, and 10 percent on truck tire service and retail.

As the company has grown, so too has its focus on the community. Cate-McLaurin has long recognized that business delivers a value that goes beyond high-quality goods and services, and has, since its founding, been consistently involved with organizations—notably the United Way—that are dedicated to community well-being.

Cate-McLaurin has been a South Carolina tradition for nearly 70 years. And its commitment to excellence—and to the character, quality, and community service that underscore everything the company does—is stronger than ever today. "I see a company where our customers say with pride that we are their tire provider," William Cate says. "Where our employees are proud of our reputation, and our public image is that of providing superior products with efficiency and integrity." Ⓒ

ᗒᑐ **Cate-McLaurin has been a South Carolina tradition for more than 60 years.**

ᗒᑐ **Character, quality, and community are the foundation of Cate-McLaurin Company, a commercial tire service firm located at 1001 Idlewild Boulevard.**

# AMERICAN ITALIAN PASTA COMPANY

American Italian Pasta Company (AIPC) produces the world's finest pasta. In fact, Columbia's own AIPC plant has the capacity to produce more than 1 million pounds of pasta a day! But the job doesn't stop there. In addition to being North America's largest pasta producer, AIPC is also a significant marketer and distributor of its products.

Established in 1988, AIPC's home base is in Excelsior Springs, Missouri, just north of Kansas City. From its earliest days, four standards have separated the company from other pasta manufacturers:

Growth and Profits: AIPC is committed to smart, vision-centered growth that creates a value for the company, its shareholders, and its employees.

People: AIPC employees are productive and efficient, and they share AIPC's dedication to producing pasta that is superior to the competition's in every way.

Quality: AIPC continually strives to ensure that its products reflect AIPC's reputation as a world leader, and does whatever it takes to sustain and build upon those standards of excellence.

Corporate Identity: AIPC seeks opportunities that reinforce its position as a leader—not only within the industry, but also among the communities and people it serves.

Where can you find AIPC's high-quality pasta? The short answer is, everywhere.

The company distributes its pasta through many outlets such as Sysco Corporation, the largest marketer and distributor of food service products. AIPC also exclusively manufactures Mueller's brand in the east and the Golden Grain brand on the west coast. AIPC supplies the majority of the largest private labels such as Publix, Winn-Dixie, Wal-Mart, and Sam's Wholesale Club and large industrial customers such as General Mills, Kraft Foods, and Pillsbury.

In order to meet the growing need for its products, AIPC has about 560 employees working in its production and distribution facilities, which are located in Excelsior Springs, Columbia, and its newest facility in Kenosha, Wisconsin. AIPC's first international pasta plant is currently under construction in Verolanuova, Italy, and is set to open in January 2001.

In February 1998, a $52-million expansion at the Columbia plant boosted AIPC's production of Bestfoods' Mueller's pasta to 45 varieties. Timothy S. Webster, President and CEO of AIPC, said the nine-month project— which brought 50 new jobs to the Columbia area—was "a monumental accomplishment and a record for the pasta industry." The Columbia plant is currently the most efficient in the nation, capable of producing in excess of 300 million pounds of pasta annually. AIPC also produces more than 80 dry pasta shapes.

While AIPC confidently looks to the future, it continues to adhere to the principles that have made the company a world leader: Sustained growth. Investment in employees who add value to the product and the process. Unparalleled quality. A fierce commitment to be the industry's best.

And if past performance points the way to future success, American Italian Pasta Company's horizon is bright indeed. 🌀

〰 **Long cut production line in Excelsior Springs, Missouri.**

〰 **Discharge of 13,000-pound-per-hour short cut production line in Columbia, South Carolina.**

# CSR HYDRO CONDUIT

South Carolina and the Midlands have seen record-breaking economic development in the last several years—but none of that growth could have happened without companies like CSR Hydro Conduit.

CSR is one of the world's largest construction and building materials groups, with operations in Australia, the United States, Asia, and New Zealand. The company is the world's largest manufacturer of quality concrete pipe, a key link to the infrastructure needed to build highways, residential areas, manufacturing plants, and retail developments.

"Nothing can be built until proper drainage is in place," said Johnny Keadle, CSR Area General Manager of South Carolina. "When you look at reports of infrastructure needs around the country, those needs just can't be met without a plant like ours."

The Columbia plant is one of over 50 CSR manufacturing facilities in the United States. In recent years CSR has added or expanded facilities in Arizona, Florida, Louisiana, North Carolina, Texas, Nevada, and Washington.

"We look forward to continued growth and expansion of our facilities throughout the country, and we're particularly excited about our growth in

South Carolina," said Bob Christensen, CSR Eastern Region Vice President.

CSR established a presence in Columbia in 1994 by buying an existing facility that had been in operation since 1974. In the spring of 2000, CSR will move into an $8-million

**Bob Christensen, Eastern Region Vice-President**

expansion at its Columbia plant, located on a 25-acre site at 300 Bill Street on the east side of town. That expansion will increase the company's production capabilities and add 15 new jobs.

That expansion will allow CSR to increase and enhance its production of 12- to 120-inch diameter concrete pipe, box culverts, three-sided bridges, and numerous specialty precast concrete products, utilized by the storm and sanitary sewer industry.

"Concrete pipe is the standard by which other materials in the industry are judged," said Keadle.

"It is the only drainage product with a life cycle of 100+ years. The strength of concrete pipe is built into the product, rather than relying on the surrounding soil."

Concrete is manufactured utilizing sand, stone, steel, and cement, making it a

**Johnny T. Keadle, Area General Manager**

very environmentally friendly product and manufacturing process.

In addition to its Columbia expansion, CSR is investing $4 million in a new facility in Myrtle Beach. This facility will supply drainage products to Myrtle Beach and the surrounding area.

CSR, with its two strategically based plants in South Carolina (Columbia and Myrtle Beach), will position itself to deliver the quality of products and services that its customers need and deserve. Currently, CSR is involved in numerous projects throughout the state, such as Interstate 26 into Charleston,

**Johnny T. Keadle, left, and Alan Boatwright. Johnny and Alan review project plans and specifications prior to bidding.**

Conway By-pass, Carolina Bays Parkway, the Bridgestone expansion in Aiken, and numerous other projects.

"We're excited about being a part of South Carolina's growth and attraction of new businesses," said Johnny Keadle. "CSR will continue investing in the future of our industry and assist in the education of professionals and the public as to Concrete Pipe and Concrete Products truly being the products of choice." 

**Project: Spring Valley Storm Drain Improvement
8' x 6' Precast Box Culvert
Engineer: SCDOT
Contractor: C. Ray Miles**

# COLITE INTERNATIONAL, LTD.

Colite International, Ltd., located in West Columbia, South Carolina, is a global supplier of architectural signage for Fortune 500 companies. Founded in 1992 by brothers Marty and Peter Brown, Colite surveys, manufactures, and installs signs in more than 50 countries worldwide. The company has established an impressive list of major clients that includes Lucent Technologies, Alcoa, Ingersoll-Rand, Bank of America, Monsanto, Siemens, Sonoco Products, Safety Kleen, Sterling Trucks, Storagetek, Alltel, ITT Industries, and Kroger.

In less than 10 years, Colite has established partnerships with other sign companies on five continents and has become a recognized leader in the worldwide sign industry. Embracing technological advances and never accepting the status quo of the industry is the secret to Colite's success.

"Because we are competing with sign companies 10 times our size, we have to be faster and better in meeting the needs of our corporate customers," says Marty Brown. "We are devoted to customer service and producing a product of superior quality, and we use technology to facilitate this process. Technology allows us to take a digital photo of a customer's present signs at their job sites, change the signs to the new designs they desire, and post the proposed designs to our web site for their approval within 24 hours. Because of our technologically advanced systems, we are able to be responsive to clients no matter where they are based."

One way that Marty and Peter Brown have been able to create their impressive global network is through memberships in local and international organizations. Early in the history of Colite, Peter Brown knew it was important to support the local burgeoning international trade association. So in 1994, Peter became the president of the Midlands International Trade Association. Peter also traveled with former South Carolina Governor David Beasley to Korea as part of a Southeast Asia trade mission. During this time, Peter and Marty traveled extensively throughout the world, both creating the groundwork of what would eventually become the largest network of sign

~ Colite International, Ltd. is a leading supplier of signage for the Fortune 500.

companies in the world. Also aiding them in their ever-expanding business was the master of international business (MIBS) program at the University of South Carolina, which has supplied them with a steady stream of marketing talent and international expertise. Marty and Peter have personally traveled to more than 35 countries and have sent their representatives all over the world, as well. They are, indeed, world-class travelers who understand international business—and this is of great benefit to their clients.

Marty is a member of the prestigious Society of International Business Fellows, based in Atlanta, and joined a class of 40 who toured China on a two-week crash course in its culture and business practices. Marty has traveled extensively throughout Europe, Asia, and particularly Central and Latin America, where Colite has founded a network of billboards—aptly called Colite Outdoor, LLC.

Marty and Peter both believe that no matter the country, business climate, or technology at hand, success is possible only with careful attention to individualized service. Colite provides this service with 52 employees who work behind the scenes in the manufacturing plant or directly with the customers in the office. Through service, quality, and innovation, and with plans for a new facility in the near future and expectations of further international expansion, Colite is supplying the world's sign needs—all from West Columbia, South Carolina. **C**

~ Peter, left, and Marty Brown, founders of Colite International, Ltd., expect to do business in over 100 countries.

Photo by Suzanne McGrane

# Chapter 13

## Business & Finance

Photo by Suzanne McGrane

# COLONIAL LIFE & ACCIDENT INSURANCE COMPANY

of accident, health, and life products. One of the leaders in the industry today, Colonial remains dedicated to providing affordable, quality products and services to its customers.

### *Putting People First—Helping Working Americans in Their Time of Need*

Based in Columbia, South Carolina, Colonial offers affordable insurance to the average working American. Colonial provides benefits solutions that help employers and employees meet their individual needs through a wide range of products, including disability, accident, and life insurance. In addition, Colonial offers special risk insurance, such as cancer and critical illness coverage. Robert Staton, chairman of Colonial, finds the most rewarding aspect of being a part of Colonial is seeing how the company helps people.

"Colonial helps working Americans in their time of need," he says. "Our insurance products provide our customers a way to protect their income against unforeseen occurrences that may happen to them."

Colonial is an industry leader in voluntary insurance benefits offered at the workplace. In fact, Colonial pioneered the concept of selling to individuals at their places of employment and allowing them to pay individual premiums through payroll deduction. In 1985, to help meet the needs of a changing workforce, Colonial began offering its portfolio of accident and health products under flexible benefits plans. Eight years later, Colonial merged with UNUM Corporation, which, through its subsidiaries, was recognized as the nation's leading provider of disability insurance products and services and a major provider of voluntary employee benefits. In 1999, UNUM merged with Provident Companies, Inc., creating the world leader in protecting the incomes and lifestyles of individuals, both directly and through their employers.

### *Putting People First—A Diverse and Supportive Work Environment*

Colonial's business is built on relationships, and those relationships are built on respect. This philosophy applies to Colonial's employees also. Colonial is dedicated to creating an inclusive work environment that respects and values the differences in the cultures, talents, and perspectives of its employees. Colonial wants to build a workforce in which individual differences are appreciated and all employees are encouraged to contribute to their fullest potential.

Colonial also recognizes the challenges its employees face in balancing their work and home commitments. That's why the company offers programs and options to help employees balance their lives. Flex time, an employee assistance program, on-site dry-cleaning service, cafeteria, postage machine, automatic teller machines, and a first-rate wellness program—including an exercise facility—are just a few of the perks employees can take advantage of—all in an effort to help them strike a balance in their overall lives.

### *Putting People First—A Commitment to Community Service*

Colonial prides itself on being a good corporate citizen, providing financial support to more than 50 organizations and projects annually, such as United Way, South Carolina Philharmonic, City Year, Communities in

〜 As one of the premier providers of employer-sponsored, voluntary employee insurance products in the nation, Colonial puts people first in everything it does—the way it serves its customers, treats its employees, and supports its community. *Photo by H. Gordon Humphries Gallery*

Putting people first. It's an axiom to live and work by at Colonial. As one of the premier providers of employer-sponsored, voluntary employee insurance products in the nation, Colonial puts people first in everything it does—the way it serves its customers, treats its employees, and supports its community.

Colonial's commitment to putting people first began with its inception in 1939, when its founding fathers, Edwin F. Averyt and J. Clifton Judy, had a vision to provide affordable insurance protection to those who needed it most—hardworking individuals and their families. In a 30-year period, they transformed their enterprise from a two-man operation selling a single accident policy for $3 into a prosperous company that offered a broad range

Schools, and Benedict College, to name a few. In fact, Colonial received the 1997 Mayor's Corporate Citizen of the Year Award because of its strong leadership role, dedication to the community, and commitment to overall citizenship. But financial support isn't the only way Colonial contributes to the community.

Colonial supports the community extensively through volunteerism. Through its "From the Heart" program, Colonial encourages employees to volunteer their time, lend their expertise, and open their hearts to those in need by helping them find opportunities for volunteering. The UNUM Foundation even matches employees' volunteer time with cash donations to the not-for-profit organization of their choice. Through its "Dollars for Doers" program, the company donates $1 to an approved not-for-profit organization for each hour of volunteer work an employee performs after the first 50 hours.

"Colonial strongly supports volunteerism, especially initiatives that help improve our schools," Staton says. "Our experiences with the South Carolina educational system have taught us how vital business and education partnerships are to our schools. We're committed to making our community a better place in which our families can work and live."

The latest chapter in Colonial's long-term support of the community is its partnership with Allendale Elementary School.

"After seeing the statistics concerning education and the overall standard of living in Allendale, we knew Colonial could and had to make a difference in the lives of these children," Staton says. "Positive adult influence is very important at this stage of a child's life, considering students mentally 'drop out' of school as early as fourth grade."

Colonial established a planning and implementation team to assess the needs of Allendale Elementary School. Based on needs, Colonial's employees have been involved in projects such as mentoring programs, hosting company tours and special events, coordinating parental outreach and recognition programs for students, teachers, and staff, and supporting teacher and staff training. ☙

∽ **Colonial supports the community extensively through volunteerism. Through its "From the Heart" program, Colonial encourages employees to volunteer their time, lend their expertise, and open their hearts to those in need by helping them find opportunities for volunteering.** *Photo by Michael Moore Photography*

∽ **Colonial is dedicated to creating an inclusive work environment that respects and values the differences in the cultures, talents, and perspectives of its employees.** *Photo by H. Gordon Humphries Gallery*

# GREATER COLUMBIA CHAMBER OF COMMERCE

"To foster an environment where businesses can flourish." This is the mission statement of the Greater Columbia Chamber of Commerce—and it's succeeding.

Eight years older than the Declaration of Independence, the Chamber of Commerce idea is one that is still relevant and necessary. Chambers were built on the belief that progress will result when men and women of high purpose work unselfishly toward common goals on various issues. The Greater Columbia Chamber of Commerce is following in that legacy.

The Greater Columbia Chamber of Commerce was founded in 1903. Projects undertaken in the early years include publishing the first city map, having the streets paved, and suggesting the creation of a local zoo. Today, the Greater Columbia Chamber of Commerce is involved in many issues related to the prosperity of the region. "The Chamber excels at building coalitions and partnerships to achieve goals that have allowed this community to experience unparalleled growth and development in the past decade," says current board of directors chairman Jack Skolds.

And what a decade it's been. An influx of international and Fortune 500 companies such as Bose, UPS, Isola, and Hueck Foils in the 1990s led to more than $1 billion in new and expanded industry. But the real story is that 60 percent of capital investment made in the region comes from existing industry. "The real barometer of a region's ability to support industry is when companies decide that growth should come in the form of expansion of existing facilities, instead of relocating," says Chamber President Donald G. "Ike" McLeese.

⌒ The Greater Columbia Chamber of Commerce serves more than 2,100 member businesses in Fairfield, Lexington, Newberry, and Richland counties.

Infrastructure development has been a crucial part of existing companies' decisions to invest in the Columbia area rather than move. The Chamber's commitment to education is part of that infrastructure mix. The Chamber has always held education issues near and dear to its heart, supporting projects such as increasing teacher salaries and the original county library plan. Today, partnerships with local educators have led to the Chamber supporting and housing the area's School-to-Work initiative, the Central Midlands Tech-Prep Consortium. One of the goals of the consortium is to ensure that area schools continue to graduate students who are well versed in technology, trainable, and understanding of the skills necessary to get and keep a job. One initiative is the organization's Teacher in the Workplace program, which places teachers in area businesses during their summer breaks. Teachers then use their experiences to create curriculum to teach necessary skills. The Chamber has been vital in creating partnerships between the schools and businesses so that the maximum number of teachers can be placed.

Developing and maintaining a sense of regionalism has been key to the Chamber's success. Once a divided community, the Columbia area has learned that cooperation can lead to great things. Chamber-sponsored coalitions and partnerships over the years led to the development of the Central Carolina Economic Development Alliance, the area's primary economic development organization; the internationally recognized Riverbanks Zoo and Botanical Garden; and plans for a regional conference center and arena that will be built jointly by local jurisdictions and the University of South Carolina.

Yet with such an active community agenda, member service remains vital to the Chamber's success. An active seminar series has helped companies

⌒ One of the Chamber's most successful programs is its annual Business Expo, the largest business-to-business trade show in South Carolina.

promote their businesses on a shoestring budget, market their products to newcomers, and even know what to expect from the OSHA inspector. Weekly Internet classes help keep companies on the cutting edge.

The Chamber is also dedicated to bringing smaller companies together for regular networking functions, such as breakfasts, after hours events, golf and tennis tournaments, and the yearly Business Expo, which has grown to become the largest business-to-business trade show in the state.

Providing programs for companies with specific needs is also important to the Chamber. Launched in 1995 to help smaller companies understand the potential of the international marketplace and to provide a roadmap to reaching those markets, the Chamber's International Trade Program was so successful that the South Carolina Chamber of Commerce took it statewide just a year after it was introduced. And the organization's Minority Business Council has created partnerships between minority-owned companies and larger corporations that have led to relationships that are beneficial to both companies.

〰 **More than 68 internationally affiliated companies, representing 16 countries, have a presence in the Columbia area.**

The council also provides a forum for minority-owned companies to discuss their needs within the community and a way to promote and strengthen minority-owned businesses.

Another jewel in the Chamber's crown is the organization's web site. With the full text of Chamber newsletters, an interactive community calendar, links to other informative web sites, and a directory of local businesses, the site provides another way for businesses to take advantage of their Chamber membership. But as the "front door to the community," the Chamber also recognizes the need to provide comprehensive information about the community, which the site does well with information about area neighborhoods, schools, hospitals, and cultural opportunities.

Member service. Community development. Partnership building. A voice for business. The Greater Columbia Chamber of Commerce is leading the way into the new millennium. ©

〰 **The Chamber provides services to member businesses including seminars, discounts, marketing, and issues awareness.**

# WACHOVIA

For instance, Wachovia was the first major bank to offer simple-interest consumer loans; also, it was a pioneer of variable-rate credit cards and the adjustable-rate mortgage, which became an industry model. In addition, Wachovia was a leader in telephone banking and the first to introduce it to South Carolina.

Thus, it is not surprising that Wachovia, the only commercial banking company ranked by millionaires among the top 10 wealth management institutions, also is a leader in cutting-edge banking technologies.

Wachovia's leadership also is rooted in public service. According to North and South Carolina Banking CEO Will B. Spence, such accountability is an important part of business. "Today, people reasonably expect businesses to share their resources for the benefit of the community," Spence said. "As a concerned corporate citizen, Wachovia contributes to economic development, education, health and wellness, and other quality-of-life areas through funding, volunteerism, public-private partnerships, and other avenues."

One Columbia-based example is Wachovia's sponsorship of the Challenger Learning Center at W.A. Perry Middle School. These centers, established in memory of the seven who died in the tragic 1986 space shuttle explosion, let students simulate Challenger's mission through exercises using math, science, and other disciplines.

Another is Wachovia's support of the arts. The bank underwrote "The Cecil Family Collects: Four Centuries of Decorative Arts from Burghley House" at the Columbia Museum of Art, significant for its landmark status as the museum's first blockbuster. Charles T. Cole Jr., executive vice president of Wachovia and president of the museum's board of directors, observed: "The arts sometimes are dismissed as a luxury; however, after only a short time in its new Main Street location, the Columbia Museum of Art has seen a tremendous increase in attendance, had a strong impact on downtown revitalization, and served many school districts through tours and programs."

Wachovia is proud to give back to the people it serves. **C**

∽ **Wachovia's leadership among financial institutions is based on a distinctive blending of stability and progressiveness.** *Photo by Robert Clark*

Trust. Stability. Trust. Soundness. Trust. At Wachovia, it all comes back to trust. Wachovia Corporation is an interstate bank holding company with dual headquarters in Winston-Salem, North Carolina, and Atlanta, serving regional, national, and international markets. Its member companies offer personal, corporate, trust, and institutional financial services. Founded in 1879, Wachovia enjoys a long history sustained by high standards and a strong commitment to customer service.

Wachovia's South Carolina operation has made important contributions to the bank's heritage and reputation. Its forerunner, the Bank of Charleston, opened in 1835, making it the state's oldest bank. In 1926, the Charleston bank merged with two Columbia institutions to form South Carolina National Bank. SCN joined the Wachovia family in 1991 and assumed the name in 1994.

Wachovia's leadership among financial institutions is based on a distinctive blending of stability and progressiveness. The bank's characteristic commitment to profitable growth ensures its strength, while forward-thinking strategies enhance Wachovia's ability to meet customers' needs and expectations.

∽ **Wachovia's leadership is rooted in public service from associates such as (left to right) Doug Kilton, Elizabeth Holstein, and Charlie Cole.** *Photo by Robert Clark*

# AGFIRST FARM CREDIT BANK

You probably wouldn't be surprised to find South Carolina's largest home-based financial institution headquartered in Columbia. But it is surprising to find that you can't walk into this bank to open a checking or savings account. In fact, the bank doesn't accept deposits.

But this $11-billion bank does serve customers in 15 eastern states and Puerto Rico—and it's been doing business in Columbia since 1917.

AgFirst Farm Credit Bank traces its history to the establishment of the Farm Credit System by Congress under the presidency of Woodrow Wilson in 1916, when the Federal Farm Loan Act established 12 Federal Land Banks. The Federal Land Bank of Columbia merged with a sister bank, the Federal Intermediate Credit Bank, to form The Farm Credit Bank of Columbia in 1988. AgFirst was born in 1995, when the Columbia bank merged with a similar institution in Baltimore, Maryland.

"The AgFirst name really embodies what we do," says Larry Doyle, AgFirst's executive vice president, lending operations. "Our primary business

∽ Columbia artist Blue Sky's famous "Tunnelvision" adorns the back wall of AgFirst Farm Credit Bank building.

is agricultural loans, and we're part of a system of banks established when farmers had a hard time getting credit from traditional banks. We were established to serve that need, and that's what we still do."

AgFirst is a wholesale bank, or financial intermediary. It doesn't lend money directly to farmers and other individuals. Instead, AgFirst's customers are 33 farmer-owned agricultural credit associations. These associations are farmer-owned and make loans for farm equipment, operations, expansions, and real estate purchases. They also make home loans to rural residents. The associations provide financial services to 85,000 customers.

"Our banking system is set up like a cooperative," said Andy Lowrey, chief executive officer and president. "When customers borrow money from a Farm Credit association, they are also buying stock in that association. In turn, the associations buy stock in a Farm Credit Bank like AgFirst that provides the funds. We then pay an annual dividend to the credit association and a portion of that goes back to the individual borrower."

The result is lower costs to farmers. The dividends can reduce interest by up to 1.5 percent over the life of a loan.

AgFirst Farm Credit Bank has a family feel to it. Many of AgFirst's employees have an agricultural background or a family history in agriculture.

"We're still close to the land, and that also means we have a real sense of community," said Doyle. "Our employees are very community-oriented. In turn, AgFirst promotes that family feeling by sponsoring annual health fairs for our employees and providing financial support to employee activities in the community."

AgFirst is also home to one of Columbia's best-known and best-loved landmarks. The bank's headquarters is graced by artist Blue Sky's mural "Tunnelvision."

"Even people who have no idea who we are or what we do know our building because of 'Tunnelvision,'" says Lowrey.

It's a unique look for a unique and valuable asset to South Carolina. ◀

∽ AgFirst Farm Credit Bank is located two blocks from Main Street at 1401 Hampton Street.

# CAROLINA FIRST

"All roads lead to Columbia," says Mack I. Whittle Jr., president and CEO of Carolina First Corporation. "Decisions affecting the people and business of this state are made daily here. As early as our founding in 1986, we knew we wanted, and needed, a presence in the capital city."

Headquartered in Greenville, Carolina First Corporation is today the largest independent bank holding company in South Carolina with assets of $3.2 billion and with 62 banking offices throughout the state and 13 banking office in northern and central Florida. Nine of those offices are in the Columbia area.

The bank has created over 300 new jobs since its arrival in Columbia in 1993. "We were determined to create a banking culture in the Midlands that serves both customers and community in a way that enhances the quality of life here," explains Mr. Whittle.

Underscoring its commitment to the capital city, Carolina First was pivotal in the 1998 Main Street revitalization, anchoring a new seven-story office building. The building serves as its Midlands headquarters, including all executive offices as well as inter-national, mortgage, trust, investments, and commercial real estate departments.

～ **Carolina First was created in 1986 with one simple yet bold mission: to become South Carolina's premier bank by putting customers first.**

the bank's lifetime. Carolina First now has more than six percent of the total banking market in South Carolina and ranks fifth in total deposit market share.

With a reputation for forging flexible and creative banking relationships, Carolina First is positioned as a super community bank, focused on serving individuals and small- to medium-sized businesses. Putting customers first is the bank's stated goal.

"When we see a need, we respond," explains Mr. Whittle. As an example, the international department was started in response to a number of the bank's small business clients who found themselves for the first time doing business overseas. Mr. Whittle concedes that it's unusual to have international banking expertise in an opera-tion the size of Carolina First, but he says, "We didn't hesitate."

Carolina First embraces change and the opportunities it provides. For instance, Carolina First holds ownership interests in both Affinity Technology Group, Inc., a developer of automated lending technologies, and NetB@nk, Inc., one of the first on-line,

Carolina First offers a full spectrum of banking services through subsidiaries: Carolina First Mortgage Company, the second-largest mortgage loan servicer in South Carolina, which is headquartered in Columbia; Blue Ridge Finance Company; and CF Investment Company, a small business investment company.

Carolina First has experienced remarkable growth with assets, loans, and deposits growing at compound rates in excess of 20 percent per year over

real-time Internet banks. Naturally, driving this interest in technology is the bank's desire to discover better ways to deliver service and products to its customers.

Part of that service involves the reinvestment of local funds into South Carolina communities. Carolina First has received several "outstanding" ratings (highest ranking) under federal community reinvestment regulations. Additionally, the bank has been recognized as the top producer in South

Carolina for the "Main Street Investment Program," a program designed to promote the growth of existing small businesses and assist in the start-up of new businesses.

"Being in Columbia keeps us more closely in touch with statewide issues that affect us and our customers," says Mr. Whittle. "It's one of the reasons we became involved in education with our Carolina 'First for Education' Foundation." The $12.6-million charitable foundation is aimed at stimulating and supporting education-related projects across the state. Carolina First also supports education through its Palmetto's Finest program, which annually recognizes South Carolina schools of excellence. ◙

# COLDWELL BANKER
# TOM JENKINS REALTY, INC.

**Top real estate company grows with community**

The Midlands has seen a steady stream of growth for many years. And for nearly a half a century, the sold sign in the front yard of thousands of Midlands homes has proclaimed Coldwell Banker Tom Jenkins Realty, Inc.

Behind the familiar blue and white sign is the company's solid position in the community. Its reputation is backed by outstanding services that homebuyers and sellers have come to trust. "That's why our clients are customers for life," said Tommy Camp, Senior Executive Vice President.

When Tom Jenkins established his company, Tom Jenkins Realty, Inc., in 1955, he had a sincere desire to see his hometown grow. And as it grew, so did his company. Jenkins saw an infinite amount of potential in becoming part of a national company that embraced a mutual commitment to customer service, professionalism, and innovation. So in 1984, the company joined Coldwell Banker Real Estate Corporation as its 800th franchise. Today, Coldwell Banker Tom Jenkins Realty operates six offices throughout Richland, Lexington, and Kershaw counties.

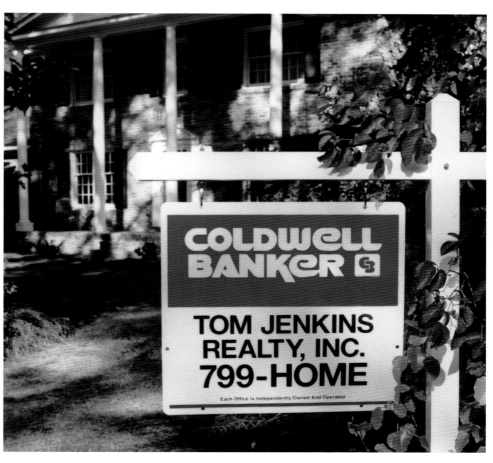

~∽ The Coldwell Banker Tom Jenkins Realty blue and white sign has become an icon representing the company's solid reputation, outstanding services, and top-rated professional associates.

Early in 1999 the company realized another opportunity for growth when it merged with Coldwell Banker Flouhouse, Realtors® in Charlotte, NC. The alliance created the "Carolinas' Connection"—a powerful team that boasts an annual sales volume of more than $1.1 billion and ranks number one among all Coldwell Banker companies in the Southeast.

The success of the company has been noted in two of the industry's leading magazines. *REAL Trends* and *National Real Estate and Relocation Magazine* ranked Coldwell Banker Tom Jenkins Realty as the Midlands' number one real estate company. Cendant Mobility Services, the world's leading relocation company, ranked Coldwell Banker Tom Jenkins Realty number one in destination services and awarded the company its elite Platinum Club status and Five-star Circle of Excellence rating.

These high ratings are achieved in two major ways—through the company's sales associates and its services.

Coldwell Banker Tom Jenkins Realty has top-rated productive sales associates who share the company's commitment to the community. The company also has the highest percentage of agents holding memberships in the Greater Columbia Association of REALTORS® Circle of Excellence.

Coldwell Banker is committed to making home buying and selling as simple as possible, using its superior one-stop-shopping services. "You don't need to go anywhere else," explained Camp. With one phone call, buyers can obtain detailed information on any Coldwell Banker listing or submit a mortgage application. They can also review all the company's listings at its

web site. "No matter how you want to find a home, we have the tools," Camp continued.

Firmly backing the blue and white sign is the company's commitment to its customers. Coldwell Banker Tom Jenkins Realty has set itself apart from its competition with its services from first contact, throughout the home search, through the closing process, to the follow-up after the sale.

Camp concluded, "Our services and our people truly make our customers, customers for life." ☙

~∽ Tommy Camp, Senior Executive Vice President

# BANK OF AMERICA

Bank of America has a rich history in the Midlands spanning seven decades through its predecessor banks, including The Citizens and Southern National Bank of South Carolina, Bankers Trust of South Carolina, NCNB National Bank of South Carolina, and NationsBank of South Carolina. Today, Bank of America offers the citizens of the Midlands the convenience of using 29 banking centers and 84 ATMs. Bank of America provides the comfort of dealing with a local bank, where the staff members provide exceptional service, and where products and prices are keenly competitive. Bankers hold broad authority to make decisions without calling headquarters. Everyone accepts responsibility to do the right thing for clients and customers. A bank whose people enthusiastically support the whole life of the community: sports, education, the arts, the undeserved. A neighborhood institution with character and history.

Now consider the even greater satisfaction that comes from a person knowing their bank also provides them with the choice, convenience, and coast-to-coast access of nationwide banking. That it is supported by thousands of sister offices, ATMs, and product and service facilities in 22 states (and the District of Columbia) from Maryland to Florida to California. That all this constitutes a banking company of such size and scope that it can (and does) spend almost $3 billion a year on technology alone, a visionary investment that, among other things, lets its customers bank how and when they want, even by phone and PC any place in the world.

As a businessperson, consider the opportunity to work with a financial services organization that can meet all financial needs. One which offers tremendous resources to small- and mid-sized businesses, corporations, and government agencies across the nation and around the world. An organization that delivers capacity and product breadth, global reach, and superior execution to each client through teams of talented professionals. One which is firmly positioned at the forefront of global finance, opening doors into

⌐⌐ 1901 Main Street, Columbia, South Carolina.

⌐⌐ Team-Bank of America's Volunteer Network.

Asia and Europe, and southward into Latin America, helping a majority of America's leading corporations compete successfully in a burgeoning global economy.

Finally, consider that all these accomplishments are just the beginning. Bank of America is determined to be much more. Its goal is to build a company that makes banking work as it never has before. A company reshaped around those things that matter most to individual and business customers: convenience, simplicity, flexibility, and dependability. A company that understands and anticipates the needs of each corporate client, responding with innovative solutions and consistently delivering knowledge, creative ideas, and excellence in execution. In short, a banking company with an outstanding global banking franchise and the best opportunity to create greater value for shareholders. ◪

# ByLaw Security and YMS

Serving in the U.S. Army provides an individual with experience in security and defense. In Ana Wallace's case, the Army also provided her with extensive experience in administration, human resource management, and operations. It is upon that sturdy foundation that ByLaw Security and Your Management Source (YMS) are built.

Many businesses, large and small, have come to depend on surveillance equipment, such as video cameras, to protect their valuables. Too often, the limitations of cameras are discovered the hard way. Valuable equipment, documents, both customers and employees can be lost or harmed due to those limitations. ByLaw Security has built its reputation for dependable, reliable security on this philosophy: an alert, well-trained ByLaw security officer has no limitations.

Before one can wear a ByLaw Security badge, he or she must undergo a comprehensive interviewing process and background check. Only the most serious in character and highest qualified earn the honor to protect clients and their valuables. After passing rigorous training certification and licensing, ByLaw security officers are placed on assignment. However, ByLaw Security prides itself on providing officers that surpass state and industry standards, so refresher training courses are taken regularly.

ByLaw security officers strive to preserve a client's peace. But if ever the peace is disturbed, they have the knowledge and ability to restore it.

After meeting strict Army standards for more than 18 years, Ana Wallace took her experience in administration and management, with a focus on accounting, business consulting, and human resource management, and started YMS. YMS is a third-party administrative company designed to enable small companies to run at their optimum levels. YMS provides management of payroll services and human resource administrative support.

As a small business owner, preparing payroll and financial statements can take too much valuable time—time which could be spent running the business and generating business growth. YMS tailors business systems to meet small business needs, reduce overhead, and alleviate technology risks. International soda companies have been using third-party administrative companies for years. Now those same services are available for small or medium businesses in the form of YMS.

ByLaw Security and YMS are businesses about people and relationships. They are businesses about reliability and dependability. Wallace prides herself on a reputation of excellence. That's why she brings respect and honesty to each client relationship. ByLaw Security and YMS have a goal for its companies and for Columbia—a better business community, a safer working environment, and a higher standard of living. 

ByLaw security officers on the steps of the South Carolina Statehouse.

Ana Wallace, CEO of ByLaw Security, represents her company at the Greater Columbia Chamber of Commerce's annual Business Expo.

# FLEET MORTGAGE

Headquartered in Columbia, Fleet Mortgage has served as an exemplary community and business leader in South Carolina for almost 20 years. The only mortgage company to rank among the top 10 national lenders for more than a decade, Fleet Mortgage's business consists of the origination and servicing of residential mortgage loans for more than 1.5 million customers across the country. The company originates loans through its retail, wholesale, correspondent, and consumer direct lending channels, as well as a relocation services company.

The bank from which Fleet Mortgage's parent, FleetBoston Financial, originated was founded in 1784. With more than 200 years of banking history, mergers, expansions, and experience, FleetBoston Financial is the largest bank in the Northeast and listed among the top 10 banks in the nation.

With this mighty parent company, Fleet Mortgage was established at 1333 Main Street (The Fleet building) in Columbia in 1985. Fleet Mortgage provides approximately 1,500 jobs to residents throughout South Carolina. The company is widely known as a generous and caring corporate citizen, and its high standards in business are consistent in its community outreach. Fleet Mortgage draws nearly half of its employees from within South Carolina and has carefully and deliberately instituted a strong volunteer program, Team Fleet, to support the mission of consistently giving back to the community.

**⌒ Headquartered at 1333 Main Street, Fleet Mortgage has been a corporate citizen in the Columbia community for 15 years.**

Team Fleet is an employee-driven volunteer group that actively participates in community programs and supports community needs. "On an individual basis, we feel it is important for each of our associates to take the time and effort to give back to South Carolina," said Bill Schenck, chairman and CEO of Fleet Mortgage. "Through Team Fleet, our associates are encouraged to express their volunteer interest and utilize their talents for the betterment of our community."

The team is composed of Fleet Mortgage employees who select and vote on the projects to which Fleet will devote volunteer time. They have successfully participated in projects for several South Carolina charities, including Habitat for Humanity, Carolina Children's Home, Cooperative Ministry, Harvest Hope Food Bank, and the March of Dimes.

In addition, Fleet Mortgage provides support for local not-for-profit organizations in the area of housing and economic development, youth and education initiatives, and culture and the arts.

Fleet Mortgage employees have consistently served on community boards throughout the years, including Columbia City Ballet, City Year, International Communications Association, Junior Achievement, River Alliance, South Carolina Women Lawyers Association, United Way of the Midlands, and The Urban League of Columbia, to name a few.

Fleet Mortgage also provides each employee with two paid volunteer days each year for active service within the community, and if employees are uncertain how and where to help, Team Fleet will facilitate a volunteer match with the employee's interests and talents.

Columbia is proud to be "home" to Fleet Mortgage—a giant in the mortgage industry and in the community. ◗

**⌒ Providing residential mortgages for over 60 years, Fleet Mortgage makes the American dream a reality for more than 1.5 million families.**

# Chapter 14

# Professions

Photo by Suzanne McGrane

# THE GILLESPIE AGENCY

*I*nteraction Powers Success is a philosophy which comes to life every day at The Gillespie Agency. Based in Columbia, The Gillespie Agency is a full-service advertising and communications firm which ranks as the Midlands' third largest according to capitalized billings (1998). The agency provides comprehensive services for a diverse group of clients. Those services include strategic planning, creative development, media planning and placement, public relations, and Internet consultation. Specifically, The Gillespie Agency provides marketing which is customized to each individual client's needs.

The Gillespie Agency was founded by Elaine Gillespie in early 1985. Today, Gillespie and business partner Rose Dangerfield lead the agency in its delivery of integrated marketing services to a host of local, regional, national, and international clients. The agency's clientele includes Ducane Gas Grills, Standard Corporation, Southeastern Freight Lines, the American Bar Association, Young Pecan Company, and BellSouth Mobility DCS. The philosophy of paying attention to detail, tailoring of services to the client's special needs, and identifying opportunities while keeping a watchful eye on budgets enables The Gillespie Agency to continue growing strong.

Straightforward thinking is one of the qualities of The Gillespie Agency's business style. Combine that with the ability to thoroughly understand a client's situation, develop effective marketing solutions, and produce award-winning, creative advertising and it's easy to understand why clients remain committed to the agency.

∾ **Elaine Gillespie, left, and business partner Rose Dangerfield lead the agency in its delivery of integrated marketing services to a host of local, regional, national, and international clients.**

Client loyalty is strong at The Gillespie Agency. One of the agency's longtime clients illustrates this best. Ducane Gas Grills, ranked 32nd in South Carolina's top 100 largest privately held companies (as compiled by Arthur Anderson, LLP, 1998), considered taking the marketing aspect of its business to a larger market after a 13-year relationship with the agency. Ducane invited The Gillespie Agency to take part in the pitch against agencies in New York, Chicago, and St. Louis. It was with sound business solutions and outstanding creativity that The Gillespie Agency demonstrated quality work can indeed be done here in the heart of South Carolina. Thus, The Gillespie Agency continues moving forward on a proven success record with Ducane, resulting in successes for both companies.

John Ducane Jr., president and CEO of Ducane Gas Grills, expresses his respect for the agency: "If the talent wasn't here, I'd go to New York. But I've been shown the talent is here. The Gillespie Agency has widened our marketing scope beyond my expectations. They are true marketing partners and continue to bring fresh perspective to our business."

The only mode of operation for employees at The Gillespie Agency is to learn every detail and live and breathe their client's world. Whether dealing with the agency president, art director, or office manager, each person is dedicated to providing the best solution for the situation at hand. And this mode of operation works.

The Gillespie Agency is deeply committed to its surrounding community as well. Pro-bono work is done year-round for organizations such as the Columbia Music Festival Association, the Richland County Sheriff's Foundation, Fine Arts Center of Kershaw County, and Aids Benefit Foundation.

Furthering that commitment to the greater Midlands, Gillespie has served on several community beautification efforts led by city and county officials, while Dangerfield is a diligent supporter and contributor to the performing arts.

Communication. Interaction. Inspiration. For a new level of insight into business and communications, The Gillespie Agency is a proven winner. **G**

∾ **The Gillespie Agency is a full-service advertising and communications firm which ranks as the Midlands' third largest according to capitalized billings.**

# SCOTT MCELVEEN L.L.P.

Gazing out the windows of Scott McElveen L.L.P.'s stylish new 12th-floor offices, a visitor can see just how dramatically Columbia's downtown skyline has changed in the last 10 years. New buildings have replaced outdated structures, and some existing structures have been remodeled to better serve a rapidly growing city.

The changes in the downtown skyline provide an appropriate analogy to Columbia's much-changed corporate environment. In today's global economy, new business procedures are constantly being created, and outdated procedures are being replaced. Companies who cannot adapt to the constant change are being left behind.

Scott McElveen, an accounting, advisory, and assurance firm based in Columbia, understands the increasing risks faced by middle-market companies. Appropriately, its goal is to provide a more sophisticated level of thinking than is available at many local accounting firms and offer the benefits and services provided by large multi-national firms at a reasonable fee structure.

"At Scott McElveen, we specialize in helping our clients define for themselves a better way to operate," says Louis McElveen, tax partner. "We offer a wide, and constantly evolving, choice of services and financial management resources geared specifically toward the best long-term interests of each individual client."

The firm started with four employees and now has more than 20 full-time employees and a client base of more than 450 clients. Keeping a constant watch on the ever-expanding metropolitan horizon, Scott McElveen has recently moved its offices to the First Union Building on Main Street.

Scott McElveen is a member firm of BKR International, the world's premier association of independent accounting firms and business advisors. BKR International is an invaluable resource for sharing current information and ideas with other leading-edge firms. It is also a member of the American Institute of Certified Public Accountants, the South Carolina Association of Certified Public Accountants, and is licensed to practice before the Securities and Exchange Commission (the highest level membership in the AICPA). Annually, the firm has an internal review, and every three years undergoes a peer review designed to evaluate Scott McElveen's total quality assurance program.

### A Wide Variety of Services

Flexibility and rapid response to change are paramount in today's fast-paced business climate. As a business resource, Scott McElveen's professional staff works together to provide client services. Such services include corporate, partnership, and individual tax planning and compliance; retirement, estate, and trust tax services; merger and acquisition planning; sales and use tax services; and litigation support and representation before the Internal Revenue Service and state tax authorities.

Business valuation services allow Scott McElveen professionals to help clients discover the true worth of a company they own or in which they have a significant interest. Audits help identify potential problem areas and top market advantages for middle-market businesses. ElderCare professionals can provide both financial and nonfinancial services. They help families plan for those golden senior years and aging.

"We built our firm on a long-term commitment to our clients," says Randy Scott, managing partner. "We devote tremendous resources toward conducting fieldwork, building a partnership with our clients, and understanding the markets in which they operate. Our clients put enormous trust in us, and we want to do everything possible to prove to them that this trust is deserved." G

**∽ Scott McElveen's eye is on the horizon. They believe companies that look to the future are companies that will thrive in this evolving world marketplace.** *Photo by George Fulton Photography*

# SAFETY-KLEEN CORPORATION

**Safety-Kleen, a local company, is the North American market leader in industrial and environmental management services with over $4 billion in assets.**

Safety-Kleen is dedicated to providing the best value available anywhere in the business of industrial and environmental waste management services through its nearly 10,000 North American employees.

Safety-Kleen's headquarters, located in Columbia, South Carolina, has close to 450 employees, and statewide it operates three service branches, one distribution center, one fuels-blending facility, one recycling center, and one secure landfill.

Safety-Kleen is the only company that offers a completely integrated network designed to collect, recycle, and dispose of an almost unlimited range of waste streams, both hazardous and nonhazardous.

### A Service Company

Safety-Kleen is first and foremost a service company. The company's 400,000 customers range in size from small-quantity waste generators to Fortune 500 companies. Safety-Kleen's infrastructure allows a broader range of services to a wide range of industries. From collection through treatment and disposal, Safety-Kleen delivers a complete environmental solution to any type of waste stream both hazardous and nonhazardous, and offers more services and capabilities from more locations than anyone else in the industry. All services are backed by a comprehensive certificate of assurance and indemnification.

Safety-Kleen's primary objective is to provide environmental/industrial services to its customers in a cost-effective, environmentally sensitive manner.

### Service Capabilities

Safety-Kleen's service capabilities are divided into two primary components: collection and recovery and treatment and disposal.

The collection and recovery component is about 80 percent of third-party revenue and includes Safety-Kleen's industrial services, and commercial and institutional services. Safety-Kleen offers the following:

- Parts Cleaner Services to both industrial and automotive customers by collecting used solvents and replacing them with clean products;
- Paint Refinishing Services, which recover paint wastes and provide paint gun cleaning services;
- Imaging Services, which include collection and recycling of silver contaminated solution from film processing;
- Oil Collections Services that recover and re-refine used lubricating oils;
- Vacuum Services that remove and dispose of sludge from underground separator tanks;
- Industrial Waste Services involving the collection and processing of drums of waste; and
- Lab Pack Services that incorporate the packing, transport, and disposal of off-spec or small quantities of unidentified wastes normally produced in laboratories, schools, hospitals, and retail establishments.

∽ **Safety-Kleen is dedicated to providing the best value available anywhere in the business of industrial and environmental waste management services through its nearly 10,000 North American employees.** *Photo by Jim Nowakowski.*

The treatment and disposal component includes thermal treatment through incineration, secure disposal in both hazardous and nonhazardous landfill sites, wastewater treatment, PCB management, and a number of specialty disposal techniques. Safety-Kleen's primary objective is to recycle.

Incinerators dispose of wastes that cannot be practically treated and reused. Safety-Kleen's incineration technologies allow safe, efficient destruction of a wide range of organic wastes.

Harbor dredging services are also included, which remove, treat, and place on shore contaminated sediments accumulated in harbor waterways.

### Environmental Programs

Safety-Kleen created the WE CARE® Program to assist its customers in attracting individuals who seek out environmentally responsible businesses. Safety-Kleen also offers compliance training to customers for their hazardous waste "cradle to grave" compliance.

Safety-Kleen is proud to have its corporate headquarters in the city of Columbia and the state of South Carolina. ◪

# CARLISLE ASSOCIATES, INC.

It's been more than 20 years since the founding of Carlisle Associates, Inc. in Columbia. Since that February day in 1977, the firm has been dedicated to extending honesty and integrity in all of its client relationships. That dedication, coupled with its highly developed skill and genuine understanding of client needs, has made it one of the most sought-after architectural-engineering firms in the Southeast.

Providing services for the industrial, commercial, governmental, and educational fields, Carlisle Associates, Inc. has grown

∾ **Arnco Corporation**

as accustomed to looking at the whole picture as it is to looking at blue prints. The team of architects and engineers provide an expansive, yet integrated, array of architectural-engineering services under one roof. From selecting a building site, to taking an ongoing role in the construction process, to consulting and maintaining safety standards for storage tank removal or air quality control, Carlisle Associates, Inc. is dedicated to delivering exactly what the client envisions. Always delivering a finished project that is attractive, adaptable, and durable.

With services available in architecture; structural, mechanical, electrical, civil, and environmental engineering; site selection, planning, and construction services; and energy conservation, you might think Carlisle Associates, Inc. is too large to provide every project with personal attention. You would be wrong. Maintaining a staff of 20 people makes Carlisle Associates, Inc. a small firm, and that has advantages. Each project is assigned a team of highly skilled professionals, and each team is assigned a project manager with overall responsibility for the project. The project manager is also the primary contact between Carlisle Associates, Inc. and the client. Since the company is small, one of the firm's principals (Jerry Friedner, PE, president and CEO or Thomas C. Carson Jr., PE, senior vice president) is always the project manager. Imagine that—the client's primary contact is a principal of Carlisle Associates, Inc. Now, that's personal attention.

The firm's list of credits includes a number of projects in the Columbia area, such as the American Italian Pasta Company, the Hulon Greene multi-family residential development, the South Carolina Criminal Justice Academy, and expansion of the Pirelli Cable North American facility. Devoting much of its skill to developing and improving the standard of life within its home state, Carlisle Associates, Inc. has developed a network of resources throughout South Carolina. Over the years, however, that network has extended its reach throughout the Southeast and into Wisconsin, Missouri, Pennsylvania, and Mexico. Thus proving that Carlisle Associates, Inc. is willing to go to great lengths to meet the client's needs and demands.

It's not the highly skilled staff or the years of experience and resources that make businesses depend and rely on Carlisle Associates for their architectural-engineering needs. It's the people, the personal attention, the respect, the knowledge, and the confidence the client receives at Carlisle Associates, Inc. that make the difference. ⬛

∾ **Viracon**

# HAYNSWORTH, MARION, McKAY & GUÉRARD, L.L.P.

For more than 100 years, Haynsworth, Marion, McKay & Guérard, L.L.P. has provided innovative legal services to businesses and individuals in the Midlands. Haynsworth, Marion, McKay & Guérard, L.L.P. has full-service offices in South Carolina's three major cities: Greenville, Columbia, and Charleston. As the oldest of South Carolina's major law firms, it represents individual, business, and nonprofit clients in all major fields of law and prides itself on providing cost-effective, creative solutions to its clients.

With over 80 lawyers and more than 100 staff, the firm has grown immensely since its founding in 1887 by H.J. Haynsworth.

Haynsworth offers a wide range of sophisticated legal services to domestic and international clients. These include the following: corporate and business, governmental, taxation, health care, litigation, worker's compensation, real estate, international and customs, tax-exempt finance, economic development, employment, immigration, construction, and environmental law.

Haynsworth attorneys frequently assist both new businesses coming to South Carolina and existing businesses which desire to expand in South Carolina with the establishment of the proper legal form of the entity, acquisition of any real estate, solutions to environmental concerns, negotiation with local and state entities regarding tax and other business incentives, and implementation of such incentives. In doing so, its attorneys have developed

a reputation for creative solutions to clients' legal needs in ever changing new areas of law.

The firm's location in Columbia, the capital of South Carolina, also makes it well positioned to interact with government officials in legal, regulatory, and legislative matters. The firm has attorneys with extensive regulatory and legislative experience in the procedures and operations of state and federal government.

As South Carolina—and especially the metropolitan Columbia region—attracts real estate and corporate investment from around the world, Haynsworth has the knowledge and resources to stay current with the ever-changing rules and regulations that can impact business conditions. The firm provides legal work for an increasing number of large, high-visibility companies.

Leadership is also based in community service. The Haynsworth lawyers are involved in the Columbia community through different organizations such as United Way, the Greater Columbia Chamber of Commerce, the YMCA soccer league, public school mentoring programs, and the Boy Scouts of America. The firm feels that service to the community is an important aspect to one's life and career. ☙

∾ **Haynsworth, Marion, McKay & Guérard, L.L.P. represents many international businesses in South Carolina.** *Photo by Sam Holland*

∾ **The firm's lawyers represent clients in state and local government matters.** *Photo by Sam Holland*

∾ **Haynsworth lawyers appear regularly before federal and state courts, including the South Carolina Supreme Court as shown here.** *Photo by Sam Holland*

# HEYWARD, WOODRUM, FANT & ASSOCIATES, LTD., AIA

Heyward, Woodrum, Fant & Associates is a small architectural firm with a history of success on projects ranging from private homes to large commercial sites—including their most recently completed project, the new Columbia Metropolitan Airport terminal. "Because we're not a large firm, we limit ourselves to a small number of commissions. That allows us to give clients our undivided attention and dedication," says Vice President Thomas Fant. "Our clients appreciate that and come back to us for future work."

Heyward, Woodrum, Fant & Associates was founded in 1964 by John Tabb Heyward Jr., who demanded the highest quality of construction and excellence in architecture. Lawrence Woodrum joined Mr. Heyward in 1973 and Thomas Fant followed in 1987. Mr. Heyward succumbed to cancer in 1995.

Mr. Woodrum and Mr. Fant are experienced in all architectural aspects and services and are known for the variety of projects they have designed and completed. "I'm more design oriented, while Thomas's strength is on the technical side, and that gives us a good balance," says firm President Woodrum. "It gives us the ability to do a wide range of work." And a wide range of work it is. Their list of clients, including The Columbia Metropolitan Airport, The Hampton Preston House, Policy Management Systems Corporation, United States Postal Service, and Mr. and Mrs. G. Larry Wilson, speaks for itself.

Although their vast experience helps Heyward, Woodrum, Fant & Associates stand beam and girder above the rest, the firm is most proud of the number of repeat clients and referrals. In fact, after completing the Columbia Metropolitan Airport redevelopment, Heyward, Woodrum, Fant & Associates was rewarded with truly unprecedented accolades—letters from visitors praising the facility's friendly design and beauty. It's testimony to the fact that the highest quality and excellence in architectural design that founder John Tabb Heyward Jr. demanded, continues today. ◙

∽ (Above) Columbia Metropolitan Airport—Concourse

∽ (Below) Policy Management Systems Corporation—Corporate Headquarters

# OGLETREE, DEAKINS, NASH, SMOAK & STEWART, P.C.

Ogletree, Deakins, Nash, Smoak & Stewart, P.C. is one of the nation's largest law firms specializing in the management side of labor and employment issues. The firm's lawyers are consistently placed among "The Best Lawyers in America," and firm shareholders include a former member of the National Labor Relations Board (NLRB), a former regional director of the Board, and a former corporate counsel for major multinational corporations.

Yet, at the firm's brand new downtown Columbia offices, talk is much more likely to center on the high premium placed on client service and satisfaction than on the firm's much-deserved accolades and impressive experience. With 150 lawyers based in offices in 12 cities throughout the country, including Houston, Chicago, and Washington, D.C., Ogletree Deakins offers a responsiveness, flexibility, and depth of knowledge simply not available at other firms.

The firm regularly files *amicus curiae* briefs with the U.S. Supreme Court on behalf of the U.S. Chamber of Commerce on important labor and employment issues. Many of the firm's lawyers regularly speak at labor and employment law seminars, and are published in the leading newsletters, trade publications, and legal education materials.

Concentrated practice groups include labor and employment law, litigation, environmental law, immigration law, employee benefits and tax law, construction and surety law, and occupational safety and health law.

"We take enormous pride in the level of experience and expertise of our partners and associates," said Eric Schweitzer, managing shareholder of the firm's Columbia office. "Our central mission is to make all of our firm's considerable resources available to every client in the most efficient means possible."

As an illustration of that mission, Schweitzer mentions a national client that needed a large team of experienced labor lawyers for an important meeting—a meeting that was taking place two days from the time of the request. Ogletree Deakins was able to assemble more than thirty experienced lawyers at the meeting, a level of responsiveness the client greatly appreciated.

"Preventive counseling" is another initiative directed toward providing superior service. Designed to produce positive business results while minimizing legal exposure, the process allows Ogletree Deakins lawyers to help the client identify workplace issues and address them before they have an opportunity to grow into litigation.

Immediate attention to client needs is critical in today's fast-changing labor climate; such an approach may be one reason why the firm counts 26 of the Fortune 50 companies within its client base. Ogletree Deakins' expertise is applied just as effectively to its smaller clients, however, some of which have but a few employees.

In an ongoing effort to ensure its characteristic high level of service, Ogletree Deakins periodically conducts client satisfaction assessments, in which clients are encouraged (anonymously) to provide candid feedback on the quality of service they receive. Responses are reviewed by the team representing the client, as well as the firm's board of directors and client services manager.

Accountability, flexibility, and experience. Ogletree Deakins has made a long-term commitment to providing the very best service to its clients—and to Columbia, one of the South's most dynamic centers of business growth. **C**

✍ Top row, from left, Dedee Rowe, Mike Brittingham, and Lewis Gossett. Bottom row, from left, Eric Schweitzer, Beth Partlow, and William Floyd.

# CHERNOFF/SILVER & ASSOCIATES

↪ **Chernoff/Silver's Columbia office was specifically designed to foster a creative atmosphere.**

At Chernoff/Silver & Associates, they know that if you don't define yourself to your critical audiences, someone else will. And it may not be the definition—or the image—you want.

For more than 20 years, Chernoff/Silver & Associates has provided advertising and public relations counsel that helps clients define themselves on their own terms.

Chernoff/Silver's history began in 1974, when Marvin Chernoff arrived in South Carolina to handle media for a gubernatorial candidate who was widely regarded as a sure loser. Within months, Chernoff had not only turned the campaign into a winner, but he had also transformed the nature of politics in the region. In 1975, he offered Rick Silver a partnership, in lieu of a salary, and Columbia-based Chernoff/Silver & Associates was born.

Today, Chernoff/Silver also has offices in Orlando and Hilton Head, and a client list of prominent regional, national, and international corporations. These clients include Shell Oil Company, The Nickelodeon Network, and others on the national level. In South Carolina, the agency currently represents SCANA, Palmetto Health Alliance, the South Carolina Education Oversight Committee, and dozens of other prominent names around the state.

Successful companies like these are looking beyond Madison Avenue and other advertising/PR hotspots for communications excellence and success.

One factor that leads these companies to Chernoff/Silver is the rarity of finding an agency that offers a full range of communications services: advertising, strategic marketing, public relations, media planning, and public affairs.

But what really sets the agency apart is the clients they've been most successful with don't see Chernoff/Silver as just their advertising or even their communications agency. To them, Chernoff/Silver is a strategic partner—equal parts sounding board, think tank, communicator, and gadfly.

"Chernoff/Silver is part of the planning process. We challenge our clients' thinking, help define and understand their audience, and then help communicate their ideas. It's unique—maybe even rare—for many companies to let an outside agency play that role. It's one we relish, and it's key to the success of our agency and, more importantly, our clients," says Rick Silver.

Finally, Marvin Chernoff says what sets Chernoff/Silver apart from other communications agencies is two things carried over from the political backgrounds of himself, Rick, and many of their associates.

"Nobody here says, 'That's not my job,' and NO deadline is impossible. We're responsive and flexible, and we have a sense of teamwork and commitment that our clients say is hard to find anywhere else," says Chernoff.

"One thing we're proudest of is our involvement in the community and in public issues," says Silver. "There's hardly a single major public issue—education reform, interstate banking, health care, and others—that we haven't played a role in in South Carolina during the last 25 years."

Chernoff/Silver recently partnered with Synergy Sports International in a joint venture called Vigor Sports Marketing and Promotion. The new company's client list already includes several NFL players such as Natrone Means and Duce Staley, professional basketball player B.J. McKie, and a number of major college basketball coaches.

In celebration of its 25th anniversary, Chernoff/Silver donated more than 85 steel palmetto trees to the Cultural Council of Lexington and Richland Counties as part of a major public art event. Local artists will decorate the trees, which will then be displayed all over the Greater Columbia area.

"We don't think there's a finer city anywhere than Columbia, and we're proud to call it our home," says Chernoff. ◧

↪ **Chernoff/Silver is located in the historic Vista in downtown Columbia.**

Chapter *15*

# Building the Columbia Region

*Photo by Suzanne McGrane*

# RUSSELL & JEFFCOAT REALTORS, INC.

Regardless of whether a Fortune 500 company or a young family of three is contemplating a move to Columbia, Russell & Jeffcoat Realtors, Inc. can be of service. The company, owned by Bob Russell, chairman of the board, and Abb Jeffcoat, president, is the Midlands' leading listing and selling real estate firm.

Founded in 1965 as Bob Russell Realty, Russell & Jeffcoat Realtors continues to grow. In fact, over the last 35 years, the company has grown from one office and a handful of agents to the area's largest real estate broker with 11 offices, over 320 sales associates, and membership in a leading national relocation network.

Today, Russell & Jeffcoat provides a wide array of specialized services to meet the needs of an expanding city and the quickly changing real estate industry. As clients rely more and more on the Internet for assistance with their real estate needs, the company's web site has become a significant resource. In order to better assist clients, new features and capabilities are added on a weekly basis.

In this age of technology, Bob Russell and Abb Jeffcoat continue to value the honest, personal service and ethics on which their company was founded. Bob Russell has often said that "a company can best be judged by its people." Russell & Jeffcoat will gladly be judged by its sales agents, an impressive group of former military officers, corporate executives, homemakers, lawyers, engineers, teachers, nurses, and other professionals. Abb Jeffcoat shares the belief in the importance of a strong sales team and the ability to meet the needs of clients. "The backgrounds of our sales agents are diverse, just like the people we serve," said Abb Jeffcoat. The company's recognition as "Best Real Estate Agency" by the readers of *The State* newspaper exemplifies the company's belief in maintaining client relationships.

A member of a leading national relocation network, Russell & Jeffcoat offers a complete program to assist families and corporate transferees through all steps of the relocation process. Each year the company helps

◠◡ **Over the last 35 years, Russell & Jeffcoat Realtors has grown from one office and a handful of agents to the area's largest real estate broker with 11 offices, over 320 sales associates, and membership in a leading national relocation network.**

hundreds of families move into or away from the Midlands area. Its affiliation with the nation's top relocation network allows for smooth moves across the state, across the country, or around the world.

When working one-on-one with families, Russell & Jeffcoat's primary goal is to handle all details while you simply get ready to move. "It seems from the moment the sign goes up, dozens of details need to be taken care of," said April Branham, marketing director. "As real estate professionals, it's our job to handle each one and get you ready to move."

While commitment is key to the success of any business, that kind of dedication is one of the elements that distinguishes Russell & Jeffcoat in the industry. "We consider ourselves ambassadors to Columbia, and we embrace that role," said Ann Miller, vice president of relocation. "Companies rely on us to show the area to potential employees who are deciding whether to move to Columbia. It's much more than looking at houses. We tour the many highlights of the area, from the university to Lake Murray."

Whether you are moving all the way from Europe or need someone to take care of the simple or even the most extravagant details of your family's move, Russell & Jeffcoat will get the job done and, bottom line, "get you ready to move." ◘

◠◡ **Russell & Jeffcoat Realtors, Inc., owned by Bob Russell, chairman of the board, left, and Abb Jeffcoat, president, is the Midlands' leading listing and selling real estate firm.**

# SMITH DRAY LINE

Back then Rex Enright was the football coach at Carolina, and Frank Howard was his counterpart at Clemson. The two in-state rivals played their game on the Thursday of the State Fair in Columbia.

The year was 1955, and Smith Dray Line's roots took hold in Columbia. Founded by Richard Guillard, the company was then known as Carolina Bonded Warehouse and was located on Greene Street. Five years later, the company became an agent for Mayflower Transit Company and was known as Carolina Mayflower. It was this move that later led to the acquisition of Carolina Mayflower by Smith Dray Line in 1971.

Smith Dray Line was founded in Greenville, South Carolina, in 1911 by Augustus Smith, who started the business with two dray horses and wagons delivering freight and steamer trunks from the railroad depot to homes and businesses throughout Greenville. Smith Dray Line became a charter agent for Mayflower Transit in 1932.

Smith Dray Line first expanded its reach outside of Greenville with the acquisition of Carolina Mayflower. Expansions into Asheville, North Carolina, and Spartanburg, South Carolina, later followed. Today, Smith Dray Line operates in six cities throughout the Carolinas with a fleet of more than 100 pieces of rolling stock. The Columbia office serves as the Southern district headquarters.

On April 15, 1991, United Van Lines extended an invitation to Smith Dray Line to join its agency family. At the time, United Van Lines was the nation's second largest carrier of household goods and the country's fastest growing van line.

"The move was beneficial to both of us," said Kirk Johnston, sales manager for Smith Dray Line. "Today, United is by far the country's largest carrier of household goods, and Smith Dray Line's business has increased dramatically because of our association."

Responding to its customers' needs, Smith Dray Line is recognized throughout the industry as a leader in commercial and institutional relocations. Smith Dray Line has handled total relocations for companies such as Blue Cross/Blue Shield, Fleet Mortgage, SCANA, BMW, and Michelin Tire.

Smith Dray Line also expanded into the records management business in 1978. The business grew so rapidly that the company started a separate subsidiary, Smith Records Management, located in west Columbia on Archives Court. Originally planned for 30,000 square feet, the building now stands at 60,000 square feet, with an expansion to 90,000 square feet in the year 2000.

The records management business spawned a new company, Information Technology Systems (ITS), which scans information from paper onto a CD-ROM.

Since Smith Dray Line has been in the Columbia area since the turn of the century, its commitment to community involvement spans a number of decades. The company is extremely involved in the Greater Columbia Chamber of Commerce, and individual employees donate their time to a number of service organizations and civic groups.

"Our employees realize how important it is to make each customer's moving experience a pleasant and successful one," Johnston said. "Whether it's a small household job or enormous company relocation, customers can count on our personal attention and outstanding service from start to finish." ◙

*Photo by Steve Cohen*

# CENTRAL CAROLINA ECONOMIC DEVELOPMENT ALLIANCE

*A Region Connected To Business*

Since 1993, a cohesive partnership has developed among the many entities involved in the industrial development process. This partnership has grown stronger each year and today the Central Carolina Economic Development Alliance (CCEDA) has become a model for other communities and regions.

Regional focus and a winning attitude describe the CCEDA. This public/private partnership was created to enhance, encourage, and foster economic development for the City of Columbia and the counties of Calhoun, Fairfield, Kershaw, Lexington, Newberry, and Richland.

Capital investments soared in 1999, totaling $756 million—the highest investment year since the establishment of the Alliance. The CCEDA has attracted nearly $3 billion in new investment from both existing and new industries who have created some 22,000 new jobs for central South Carolina residents. These numbers reinforce the fact that this is a great place for business. The economic results and number of world-class companies locating in the region prove that the CCEDA team is making a difference with a spirit and desire for success.

According to South Carolina Department of Commerce Secretary Charles S. Way Jr., "One of the most important benefits of the Alliance is its ability to perform as one entity—a seamless business team—working to benefit the entire area and increase prosperity for everyone."

∽ **The CCEDA has attracted nearly $3 billion in new investment from both existing and new industries who have created some 22,000 new jobs for central South Carolina residents.** *Photo by Brian Dressler*

What is the CCEDA secret to success? Actually, it's pretty simple, and it makes good business sense. They market the region collectively. And the region has a lot to market:

- Strategic east coast location
- Trained, skilled workforce
- Excellence in education
- Thriving arts community
- Superior transportation options
- Close proximity to the Port of Charleston
- Pro-business government
- Diverse economic structure
- Exceptional lifestyle

Also, with the assistance of the CCEDA, industrial prospects can stream-line a variety of site-selection concerns. The CCEDA offers a broad range of services that ease the decision-making process. **C**

# CLYDE NETTLES ROOFING AND PAINTING

For more than 50 years, people throughout Columbia and the surrounding area have relied on Clyde Nettles Roofing and Painting for outstanding quality in commercial and residential roofing, painting, and carpentry services. Customers know that the Clyde Nettles name means not only an expert job done right, but also a guarantee of satisfaction no matter the time it takes.

Established in 1950 by Clyde Nettles, the company is still family-owned and operated today by the Porth family. Neclause Porth worked side-by-side with Clyde and Sabin Nettles as a painting contractor from the earliest days of the business, eventually bringing in his sons to work with him. Neclause Porth's sons Tony, Albert, and Jamie purchased the business when Mr. Nettles retired in 1983, with a promise to maintain the pride in the Nettles name so carefully built throughout the years.

Today, Clyde Nettles Roofing and Painting employs approximately 50 people and handles commercial and residential projects, with divisions including Commercial Painting, Residential Painting, Roofing, and Carpentry. The company acts as a subcontractor on large commercial jobs, and hires smaller, independent professionals as subcontractors for residential projects.

The majority of the work of the Commercial division is painting in new construction such as shopping centers and office buildings. The company recently was selected for such notable painting jobs as the new National Advocacy Center at the University of South Carolina, the Post Office's Southeastern Distribution Center, which covers nine acres, and the Seacoast Medical Center, a 100,000-square-foot medical facility in Little River, South Carolina.

The Residential division handles every aspect of home repair and improvement, including exterior and interior painting, roofing, and carpentry for remodeling or repairs. The company is experienced at insurance repairs

☙ **Clyde Nettles Roofing and Painting, a mainstay in the Columbia roofing, painting, and carpentry repair business for many years, employs approximately 50 people in the area.**

for fire and water damage, including replacing carpeting, tile, and household fixtures. Clyde Nettles Roofing and Painting also can handle more extensive damage repairs.

"Even if a resident has to move out due to extensive damage, we can come in and gut a house, totally remodel it in all aspects, and will even vacuum and lock up the front door then hand you the keys," says Paul Lancaster, who has worked for the company for 17 years, in just about every department. "We don't just go in and put a band-aid on your problem," he says. "For example, if you call us in because you have water spots on the ceiling, we don't just fix the spots and go home. We come in and find out why you have water spots, where the water is coming from, and fix that, and then fix the spots."

It's that kind of attention that has kept the Clyde Nettles name and reputation solid for so many years. And that attitude—a concern for the details and an emphasis on quality above all else—carries through to every aspect of the business, says company President Suzette Porth. "Our employees are talented individuals who are good at the work they do and are proud of it," she says. "We don't cut corners. If we make a mistake, we fix it the right way. That's how we keep our reputation, our employees, and our customers." ☙

☙ **Clyde Nettles Roofing and Painting has a solid reputation for quality work, experienced and reliable employees, and complete customer satisfaction.**

# ENTERPRISE INDEX

**Adam's Mark Hotel Columbia**
1200 Hampton Street
Columbia, South Carolina 29201
Phone: 803-771-7000
Toll-Free: 800-444-ADAM
Fax: 803-254-2911
www.adamsmark.com
*Page 166*

**AgFirst Farm Credit Bank**
1401 Hampton Street
Columbia, South Carolina 29201
Phone: 803-799-5000
Fax: 803-254-1776
E-mail: mstiles@agfirst.com
www.agfirst.com
*Page 197*

**American Italian Pasta Company**
2000 American Italian Way
Columbia, South Carolina 29209
Phone: 803-695-7300
Fax: 803-695-7400
www.aipc.com
*Page 186*

**Bank of America**
1901 Main Street
Columbia, South Carolina 29201
Phone: 803-765-8011
E-mail: relocation.services@bankofamerica.com
www.bankofamerica.com
*Page 200*

**BellSouth**
P.O. Box 752
Columbia, South Carolina 29201
*Page 174*

**Benedict College**
1600 Harden Street
Columbia, South Carolina 29204
Phone: 803-253-5132
Fax: 803-253-5255
E-mail: hunterk@benedict.edu
www.benedict.edu
*Pages 146*

**Blue Cross and Blue Shield of South Carolina**
I-20 at Alpine Road
Columbia, South Carolina 29219
Phone: 803-788-3860
www.southcarolinablues.com
*Page 152*

**ByLaw Security and YMS**
1125 Pope Street
Columbia, South Carolina 29201
Phone: 803-771-4175
Fax: 803-771-8979
E-mail: mgtsource@aol.com
*Page 201*

**Carlisle Associates, Inc.**
1015 Gervais Street
P.O. Box 11528
Columbia, South Carolina 29211
Phone: 803-252-3232
Fax: 803-799-9054
E-mail: carlisleassociates@carlisleassociates.com
www.carlisleassociates.com
*Page 209*

**Carolina First**
P.O. Box 12249
Columbia, South Carolina 29211
Phone: 800-476-6400
www.carolinafirst.com
*Page 198*

**Cate-McLaurin Company**
1001 Idlewild Boulevard
Columbia, South Carolina 29201
Phone: 803-799-1955
Fax: 803-343-3486
E-mail: catem@usit.net
www.catemclaurin.com
*Page 185*

**Central Carolina Economic Development Alliance**
930 Richland Street
Columbia, South Carolina 29201
Phone: 803-733-1131
Fax: 803-733-1125
E-mail: dking@cceda.org
www.cceda.org
*Page 218*

**Chernoff/Silver & Associates**
801 Gervais Street
Columbia, South Carolina 29201
Phone: 803-765-1323
Fax: 803-765-1485
www.chernoffsilver.com
*Page 213*

**Clyde Nettles Roofing and Painting**
7524 Fairfield Road
Columbia, South Carolina 29203
Phone: 803-754-0986
Fax: 803-754-0997
*Page 219*

**Coldwell Banker Tom Jenkins Realty, Inc.**
1136 Washington Street, Suite 700
Columbia, South Carolina 29201
Phone: 803-799-HOME
Fax: 803-733-3693
E-mail: cbtjr@tjr.com
www.tjr.com
*Page 199*

**Colite International, Ltd.**
P.O. Box 4005
West Columbia, South Carolina 29171
Phone: 803-926-7926
Fax: 803-926-8412
E-mail: colite@msn.com
www.colite.com
*Page 188*

**Colonial Life & Accident Insurance Company**
1200 Colonial Life Boulevard
P.O. Box 1365
Columbia, South Carolina 29202
Phone: 803-798-7000
www.unum.com/colonial
*Page 192*

**Columbia Metropolitan Airport**
3000 Aviation Way
West Columbia, South Carolina 29170
Phone: 803-822-5000
Toll-Free: 888-562-5002
Fax: 803-822-5141
E-mail: colaarpt@logicsouth.com
www.columbiaairport.com
*Page 170*

**The Country Club at WildeWood and Woodcreek Farms**
90 Mallet Hill Road
Columbia, South Carolina 29223
Phone: 803-788-4842
Fax: 803-699-2451
www.woodcreekgolf.com
*Page 167*

**CSR Hydro Conduit**
300 Bill Street
Columbia, South Carolina 29209
Phone: 803-776-6769
Fax: 803-776-2382
E-mail: jkeadle@csra.com
*Page 187*

**Embassy Suites**
200 Stoneridge Drive
Columbia, South Carolina 29210
Phone: 803-252-8700
Fax: 803-256-8749
www.embassysuites.com
*Page 158*

**Fleet Mortgage**
1333 Main Street
Columbia, South Carolina 29201
Phone: 800-458-6639
Fax: 803-929-7899
E-mail: corporatecommunications@fmgc.com
www.mortgage.fleet.com
*Page 202*

**Galeana Chrysler-Plymouth-Jeep-Kia**
180 Greystone Boulevard
Columbia, South Carolina 29210
Phone: 803-779-7300
Fax: 803-251-2086
E-mail: galeanasc@mindspring.com
www.galeanasc.com
*Page 162*

**The Gillespie Agency**
3007 Millwood Avenue
Columbia, South Carolina 29205
Phone: 803-779-2126
Fax: 803-254-4833
E-mail: elaine@thegillespieagency.com
www.thegillespieagency.com
*Page 206*

**Greater Columbia Chamber of Commerce**
930 Richland Street
Columbia, South Carolina 29201
Phone: 803-733-1110
Fax: 803-733-1149
E-mail: info@gcbn.com
www.columbiachamber.com
*Page 194*

**Haynsworth, Marion, McKay & Guérard, L.L.P.**
1201 Main Street, Suite 2400
Columbia, South Carolina 29201
Phone: 803-765-1818
Fax: 803-765-2399
E-mail: egkluiters@hmmg.com
www.hmmg.com
*Page 210*

**Heyward, Woodrum, Fant & Associates, Ltd., AIA**
4910 Trenholm Road, Suite A
Columbia, South Carolina 29206
Phone: 803-790-4666
Fax: 803-790-0786
E-mail: tfant9052@aol.com
*Page 211*

**IMIC Hotels**
One Surrey Court
Columbia, South Carolina 29212
Phone: 803-772-2629
Fax: 803-750-8478
E-mail: sryan@imichotels.com
www.imichotels.com
*Page 164*

**Midlands Technical College**
P.O. Box 2408
Columbia, South Carolina 29202
Phone: 803-738-8324
Fax: 803-738-7784
E-mail: mtcinfo@mtc.mid.tec.sc.us
www.mid.tec.sc.us
*Page 154*

**Ogletree, Deakins, Nash, Smoak & Stewart, P.C.**
1501 Main Street, Suite 600
Columbia, South Carolina 29201
P.O. Box 11206, 29211
Phone: 803-252-1300
Toll-Free: 888-548-1300
Fax: 803-254-6517
E-mail: columbia@odnss.com
www.ogletreedeakins.com
*Page 212*

**Palmetto Health Alliance**
P.O. Box 2266
Columbia, South Carolina 29202-2266
Phone: 803-296-2000
Fax: 803-296-5335
www.palmettohealth.org
*Page 148*

**Providence Hospital**
2435 Forest Drive
Columbia, South Carolina 29206
Phone: 803-256-5300
www.provhosp.com
*Page 150*

**Russell & Jeffcoat Realtors, Inc.**
1022 Calhoun Street
Columbia, South Carolina 29201
Phone: 803-779-6000
Fax: 803-343-2602
E-mail: rjinc@russellandjeffcoat.com
www.russellandjeffcoat.com
*Page 216*

**Safety-Kleen Corporation**
1301 Gervais Street, Suite 300
Columbia, South Carolina 29201
Phone: 803-933-4200
www.safety-kleen.com
*Page 208*

**SCANA Corporation**
1426 Main Street
Columbia, South Carolina 29201
Phone: 803-217-9000
E-mail: clove@scana.com
www.scana.com
*Page 172*

**Scott McElveen L.L.P.**
1441 Main Street, Suite 1200
Columbia, South Carolina 29201
P.O. Box 8388, 29202
Phone: 803-256-6021
Fax: 803-256-8346
www.scottmcelveen.com
*Page 207*

**Smith Dray Line**
P.O. Box 3247
Columbia, South Carolina 29230
Phone: 800-332-5673
Fax: 803-754-4892
E-mail: kirk.johnston@smithdray.com
www.smithdray.com
*Page 217*

**Time Warner Cable**
Columbia, Orangeburg & Sumter
293 Greystone Boulevard
Columbia, South Carolina 29210
Customer Service: 803-252-2253
General Administration: 803-251-5300
www.sc.rr.com
*Page 175*

**United Parcel Service**
124 Creekside Road
West Columbia, South Carolina 29172
www.ups.com
*Page 182*

**USC College of Engineering & Information Technology**
Swearingen Engineering Center
University of South Carolina
Columbia, South Carolina 29208
Phone: 803-777-4259
Fax: 803-777-3233
E-mail: info@engr.sc.edu
www.engr.sc.edu
*Pages 144, 180*

**Wachovia**
1426 Main Street
17th Floor/SC 8502
Columbia, South Carolina 29226
Phone: 803-765-3164
Fax: 803-765-3134
E-mail: financial.solutions@wachovia.com
www.wachovia.com
*Page 196*

**Westinghouse Nuclear Fuel Business Unit**
5801 Bluff Road
Columbia, South Carolina 29209
Phone: 803-647-3208
Fax: 803-695-4152
E-mail: loveleja@westinghouse.com
*Page 184*

**Woodcreek Farms**
1712 Woodcreek Farms Road
Elgin, South Carolina 29045
Phone: 803-865-3276
Fax: 803-865-7290
E-mail: jembroker@aol.com
www.woodcreekgolf.com
*Page 167*

**YMCA**
1420 Sumter Street
Columbia, South Carolina 29201
Phone: 803-799-9187
Fax: 803-799-2897
E-mail: uptown@columbiaymca.org
www.columbiaymca.org
*Page 153*

# BIBLIOGRAPHY

Central Carolina Economic Development Alliance, annual report, 1997.

*Central Carolina Business Review & Investment Guide*, Greater Columbia Chamber of Commerce, 1997.

*Central Carolina: An Executive Summary*, Central Carolina Economic Development Alliance, 1997.

"Columbia's Master Plan Includes the Vision of Many," *Greater Columbia Business Monthly*, June 1997.

"Cooperation key to plan for area development," *The State* newspaper, November 25, 1997.

"Gervais Streetscape, Traffic flowing smoothly," and "Vista grows in diversity, Economic development key aspect," *Cityscape* magazine, Winter 1998.

"Harbison's Newest Project: Columbiana Station," *Greater Columbia Business Monthly*, December 1997.

"The Lykes Building Regains Its Old Glory" and "Old Armory Gets New Life," *Greater Columbia Business Monthly*, October 1997.

O'Shea, Margaret N., "River's History Saved?" *The State* newspaper, November 5, 1997.

*Regional Guide to Greater Columbia*, Greater Columbia Chamber of Commerce, 1997.

# ACKNOWLEDGEMENTS

A special thanks to James Quantz Jr., who provided additional photography. He is a native of Columbia who specializes in large-format and scenic photography.

The author also wishes to acknowledge information acquired through interviews with Ray Sigmund of the Columbia Historic Preservation Society, Jim Gambrell of the Columbia Economic Development Office, and Crystal Hampton, preservation zoning coordinator.

Additional facts were obtained from The River Alliance, *South Carolina Wildlife Magazine,* The Saluda Shoals Foundation, the University of South Carolina Information Department, and various Web sites, including the home pages of the City of Columbia, Palmetto Health Alliance, Lexington Medical Center, Providence Hospital, and the University of South Carolina.

Historic photographs were provided by the University of South Caroliniana Library, University of South Carolina, Columbia.